MIND

over

MONEY

MANAGEMENT

Strategies Your Financial
Advisor Won't Give You

**How To Make Money Work For You,
Get Out Of Debt, Relieve Stress and
Make Financial Planning Simple**

Crane Publishing
116 Hazley Ave
Rochelle Park, NJ 07662
www.RobynCrane.com
(800) 273-1625

To get book bonuses and updated
versions of the book, go to:
www.robyncrane.com/bookbonuses

Third Edition

Kindle Edition 2015
Published in The United States Of America

Ordering Information:

Quantity sales. Special discounts are available on quantity purchases by corporations, associations, and others. For details, contact the publisher at the address or phone number above.

Orders by U.S. trade bookstores and wholesalers. Please contact: support@robyncrane.com or Tel: (800) 273-1625.

Photo Credits
Ambur Cole Photography

CONTENTS

CONTENTS 3

DEDICATION 1

WHAT TO EXPECT 3

INTRODUCTION 7

SPECIAL GIFT..25

PART I: WHERE YOU ARE 27

STEP 1 ~ KNOW YOUR MONEY TYPE...................29

STEP 2 ~ UNCOVERING YOUR MONEY MaSK™ 61

STEP 3 ~ TRACK YOUR NET WORTH....................71

PART II: WHAT'S HOLDING YOU BACK 79

STEP 4 ~ FACE YOUR ISSUES 81

STEP 5 ~ ACKNOWLEDGE YOUR LIMITING BELIEFS................95

PART III: WHERE YOU WANT TO BE 107

STEP 6 ~ DETERMINING WHAT YOU WANT 109

STEP 7 ~ ESTABLISH AND MAINTAIN A SYSTEM 123

STEP 8 ~ SET TARGETS 143

PART IV: GETTING WHAT YOU WANT 165

STEP 9 ~ TAKE APPROPRIATE ACTION 167

STEP 10 ~ SET YOURSELF UP FOR SUCCESS 185

CONNECT WITH ROBYN 207

FREE RESOURCES..208

WHAT TO DO NEXT 209

WORKING WITH ROBYN 211

BOOK ROBYN 213

ABOUT THE AUTHOR 215

DEDICATION

To my honey and hubby, Trevor
To my favorite daughter, Phoenix
To my precious dog, Moxie
To my mom, dad, brothers, and all my besties
To all my clients for teaching me how to be a better coach
To you, for trusting me to help you master your money

WHAT TO EXPECT

Dear Friend,

Welcome to ***Mind Over Money Management****: Strategies Your Financial Advisor Won't Give You.*

This book represents some of the most valuable life lessons and insights I've had throughout my life. It represents years of hard work, struggle, and experience from not just me, but from the efforts of my incredible team and clients. Possibly... you're one of them! (If you are, thank you!)

Before you dive in, I wanted to take a moment to share some thoughts with about what to expect in this book.

<u>First, it's interactive.</u>

There are many opportunities for you to dig deeper into the content, and gain access to several free training videos, workshops, templates and bonuses, as well as ways you can participate in some interactive LIVE events. You will also be given a chance to register to get updates to this book as I continue to improve and expand it. (<u>www.robyncrane.com/bookbonuses</u>)

<u>Second, I also want you to know that I know that this book is not perfect.</u>

I humbly accept that there may be some inevitable errors, grammar or possibly spelling mistakes, inside this masterpiece. In fact, if you find any mistakes, PLEASE tell me by sending the error and page you found it on to my team at support@robyncrane.com. Thanks in advance.

Third, please USE this book.
Write in it. Do the exercises...

If you have a physical copy - write in it. If it's a digital version, and you know how to highlight and take notes - do it. Often times in the following pages, I'll ask you to write things down. So take out your journal, or notebook, or print out the pages—whichever you do, PLEASE do the exercises I recommend, even if they seem silly. Even if you think you don't *really* need to. Even if you don't want to.

This book is for implementers. You'll see there are tons of ideas that you can use, regardless of your situation right now, whatever it is. If you're the type who's looking for free and easy, with no work... then this isn't the book for you.

Fourth, this is not an investment book

This book doesn't teach you how to invest, what to invest in or how to grow the money you already have. Unfortunately, most people's biggest problem with money is that they don't have much of it. So this book focuses on **you**, the only real thing determining your wealth.

You may have heard the adage, "It's not how much money you make that matters, it's how much you keep."

Following the strategies in this book can absolutely help you keep more money, and once you can do that growing your money can be very simple.

Lastly, this book wasn't intended
to be a NY Times #1 Bestseller.

Instead, it was designed to start a conversation with you, and give us a chance to get to know each other better, develop trust, and a bond and ultimately help us decide if we should work together someday.

My intention for you and the purpose of this book is to show you the most powerful ways you can transform your life.

Don't be a stranger! Leave a comment on my Facebook page so after you get to know me through the pages, I'll get to know you too.

I'm looking forward to getting to know you better!

Enjoy,

Robyn Crane

PS - As you delve into the book and your life begins to transform, I'd absolutely, positively **love** to hear from you. Specifically, I'd love to hear about the challenges you've had, and have now overcome since applying the tools in this book. Please leave a comment, or better yet, post a picture or video on my Facebook wall at: https://www.facebook.com/moneyandrelationships.

INTRODUCTION

<u>Mind over Money Management</u>

Your mind is very powerful. How you think determines how you feel—and how you feel determines what you choose to do (or not to do)—which of course, affects your money.

I don't need to convince you of the power of the mind. Nor do I need to convince you that shifting your mindset could absolutely shift your finances. You've likely heard it before or perhaps read it in Napoleon Hill's, *Think And Grow Rich*.

So, if you believe this is true—that shifting your mindset can help you make more money and get out of debt, and help you save money or give you the feeling of peace-of-mind instead of stress about money, then why don't you have it?

If you're anything like the people who call into my radio show, appear on my TV show, or the clients who hire me, you might be asking yourself, *"How do I change my mindset?"* or *"How do I shift my beliefs?"* or *"How do I stop having bad money habits?"*

The answer is, you need to "train your brain." It may sound a little wacky, but trust me on this.

So how do you "train your brain?" The specific, "How To's" are laid out for you in this book in 10 easy steps.

In a nutshell, though, you "train your brain" by making small shifts in your beliefs or your behaviors, or both.

Look, you've had beliefs about money since you were a little kid. These beliefs influenced your behaviors. And whether you're rich or poor, whether you have a lot of money or a lot of debt, and whether you feel great or terrible about your money— all is determined by these two factors: your beliefs and your behaviors.

As I teach in my seminars,

Beliefs + Behaviors = Bank Account

I use "bank account" loosely to refer to your money (because as you can see, I needed another "B"). These are the three B's of the Money ABCs, also known as the 3 Formulas of Money Attraction.

I teach these principles in depth in my *Money Mastery Coaching Program*. (Get the free overview here at: www.RobynCrane.com/moneyattraction)

What's incredible about this formula is that it actually works as a "Crazy 8."

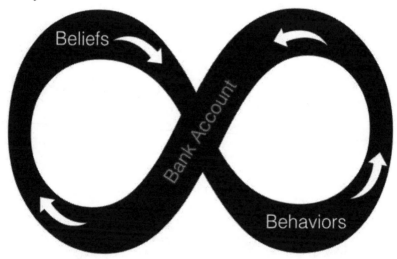

Your beliefs *absolutely* influence your behaviors, which affect your bank account.

Let's say you believe that "rich people are greedy." Don't you think that this will affect your behaviors? Of course it will. Maybe you'd overspend, maybe you'd sabotage job interviews, maybe you'd take big risks when investing and then lose it all—just so you won't be seen as greedy. Even though you might say you want more money, if your beliefs or behaviors aren't aligned with that, your "bank account" will scream, "LIAR!"

But check this out.

Here's how this you can change your life and use the "Crazy 8" to your benefit.

When you shift any one of the B's, it affects the others, so if you change the belief "rich people are greedy" to "rich people are generous," it will shift your behaviors. This will ultimately change your bank account.

Likewise, when you change your behaviors, like tracking your money in a specific way (detailed in Steps 2, 3 & 7), this behavior can lead you to making more, or spending less. You will then begin to notice that as your beliefs change, so does your bank account. All of you sudden, you might have new beliefs like, "**I** am in control my financial destiny" or "financial planning **is** easy."

And when your bank account changes, the whole glorious cycle perpetuates itself.

As empowering as this idea can be, this is also exactly why your beliefs or behaviors could have you spiraling into a whirlpool of debt, or why you may have little to show for yourself at 55 years old after working for 30 years, or why you feel stressed about money no matter how much money you have.

The 10 steps in this book (given to you in a fun and easy-to-apply way) will help you recognize and shift disempowering beliefs and behaviors, so you can master your money and have the life you want and desire.

Strategies Your Financial Advisor Won't Give You

Most financial advisors help you invest money you've already saved or invest any extra money you have left over at the end of the month. But if you're like most people, even though you work hard and make decent money, being able to save money is just as big of a problem as being able to manage it.

Traditional financial planning and retirement planning don't help much when you're struggling to pay the bills or racking your brain to figure out how to get out of debt.

Maybe you have a financial advisor, and maybe you don't. Either way, the principles in this book will help you keep more of what you make, so if and when you do want to hire a financial advisor, you'll actually have more money to invest and make money work for **you**.

It's not that your financial advisor (if you do have one) is intentionally withholding this valuable information from you. It's just that, tragically, what I cover in this book is simply not part of the traditional financial planning "curriculum."

Nope, your typical financial advisor won't give this to you. And the reason is that they simply weren't taught this stuff. I know this, because I'm a financial advisor.

Before I became a financial advisor, I thought financial advisors were greedy. I would have never guessed that I'd become a financial advisor in a million years. I wanted to help people and make a difference in this world. I didn't care about making a lot of money, which is what I thought financial planning was all about.

Then, in October of 2006, I got a random call for a job interview with a financial planning company. I almost hung up the phone. By the end of the call, I decided to go to the interview for two reasons:

1) I needed the practice. (I had only had one other job interview in my life), and 2) it was on the way to where I was already driving the same day of the interview.

As I walked into a room full of 12 people in suits, I started immediately regretting my decision. My previous "business" experience, which you'll learn about shortly, did <u>not</u> prepare me for this. I had never made more than $20,000 per year, I never had a "real" job in my life and my financial knowledge barely included the basic definition of a mutual fund.

However, one young woman, named Maria, changed my attitude and my life. She presented the opportunity to become a financial advisor with poise and passion. She said, "Financial planning will allow you to help people send their kids to college, buy a house and retire."

My belief about financial advisors being greedy changed in an instant. All of a sudden I thought of this new and unfamiliar profession as something noble.

The next thing I knew, I took the job. No experience? No problem. No education? No worries. But there was a catch: There was also no salary. Commission only. Ouch.

However, I figured that if all I got from this experience was financial knowledge, I could at a minimum improve my own financial situation, and that in itself seemed worth the investment.

Six weeks and several exams later, I was a financial advisor. As part of the job, I started recommending mutual funds and insurance products to help people change their lives. I had to disregard the doubting voice in my head that said, *"Who am I to tell them what to do?"* and instead just trust the system. But it was a little scary.

They didn't train us how to teach clients how to manage their money, or how to make more money, or how to get out of debt.

Instead, we were taught "product knowledge," and how to sell.

Most definitely, we didn't learn anything about how to teach clients to adjust their *beliefs* or *behaviors* so that they could have more money to build their wealth.

Nonetheless, I felt great because I felt like I was helping people. Even though my job turned out to be a sales job, if I hadn't felt that what I was doing was impacting people's lives, I would have quit immediately.

The first two years were great. I was helping people save towards their goals. They were happy and so was I.

However, in 2008—the market crashed, and I watched my clients' accounts go down extremely fast. And I did what most financial advisors did. I used the "buy and hold" investment strategy. I bought mutual funds for them and did not sell them as the market plummeted. This meant my clients' accounts dropped over 50% in less than a year.

My life changed again shortly after the market bottomed in March 2009. I attended a presentation where an unconventional financial advisor spoke about how *typical* financial advisors put their clients in costly products and don't know how to protect and grow their money.

As I sat in the room listening to this financial advisor speak, my heart sank and I got sick to my stomach. I was fighting to keep the tears from dripping down my face. I was thinking to myself, *"Am I one of those typical financial advisors? Am I hurting my clients instead of helping them? Could I have prevented them from losing all that money?"*

It was then and there that I decided that I'd be willing to do whatever it takes to gain more knowledge and become a true expert in my field. I decided to invest more in my own personal growth and in learning in-depth financial education outside of the traditional financial planning arena so I could help my clients as much as humanly possible.

I did this by investing every dime I had (and often "dimes" I didn't have) into my education. Over the years, I've invested well over $100,000 in books, products, programs, and seminars—not to mention several private coaches, experts and consultants, so I could not only improve my own life, but also truly help my clients transform theirs.

The strategies in this book are not strategies a financial advisor would give you to invest your money, or even plan for retirement. (That's content for another book.) ☺

However, everything you learn in this book can definitely affect how much you have to invest, how much you have to save for retirement, and countless other areas of your finances and your life.

For example, some of my newest clients applied just a few of these strategies over the last month, and they're already having transformational results.

In just one month, one lovely couple, let's call them Greg and Kim went from overspending $1700 when we began working together to keeping $2700 the following month.

This means they were going in the hole by $1700 (and I'm pretty sure this wasn't the first or only month). That's a NEGATIVE $1700 that they were losing before they started following my system. And in their first month, they instead had $2700 left over—that's a $4400 spread! This is extra money they now have to put towards paying down their debt or towards an emergency fund or any other goal they desire.

They did not do this by investing in any way. They did it simply by changing their money behaviors. (We haven't even made any effort towards shifting their money beliefs yet, and I'll explain why that matters later in the book.)

But, wouldn't you agree intuitively that by getting these incredible results, like watching their bank account grow so much in such a short period of time, might impact their beliefs! Well, it did!

Greg and Kim now believe without a shadow of a doubt that they can get out of debt, get on track for retirement and even have a better relationship!

And even though, they had to cut back on expenses in order to make this happen, they actually felt like their quality of life got better, not worse! Isn't that awesome?

No mutual fund, no matter what the return, will ever make you feel like this!

With the knowledge you'll get from reading this book, and most importantly by applying my 10 steps, you will be able to build a solid foundation of empowering money habits that no bad investment or stock market crash can ever take away.

Overcoming Your Money Issues

If you want to learn how to make money work for you, get out of debt, relieve your money stress and make financial planning easy, then pat yourself on the back. You have the right book in your hands.

This book is for you if you want to improve every area of your life by making one simple decision. The decision to face your money issues -- head on.

In order to get transformational results like I just mentioned, you must begin by overcoming your money issues.

Deep down, you know that your money issues hold you back. This may not keep you up at night and you may have learned to exist pretty contently in spite of it, but in your heart of hearts, you're not achieving your full potential and your life is much more stressful, and less abundant than it could be if you had mastery over your money.

You may overspend it, hoard it, give it away to others, buy items you can't afford or just avoid it, burying your head in the sand. Whatever it is you're doing (or not doing), you're not on track to wealth or managing your money the way you'd like to be. But maybe you're not sure how to change or you just can't seem to get motivated.

If you have an inkling that the way you handle, or don't handle money trickles down into every area of your life, you're absolutely right. If you're not fully present to that yet, this book will reveal the simple truth that as you shift your mindset and improve your relationship with money, you will have the ability to transform your life.

You see, your relationship with money affects everything else in your life. You probably don't stop and think about it, but all of your relationships are greatly impacted by money: Your relationship with your boss or business, your spouse, kids, parents, siblings, friends, and even your health, spirituality, and recreation.

No matter how bad, good, or even *great* your relationship with money is, that relationship is *always* there.

Here are some examples of what I mean: You don't feel you are getting paid what you're worth, so you resent your boss and your performance starts to tank. Your spouse doesn't let you in on money matters, so you feel confused and frustrated. Your parents lent you money in a moment of need and you feel embarrassed and ashamed that you haven't been able to pay them back yet. Your younger sibling is always mooching off of you, so you avoid him like the plague. Your friends invite you out to dinner and you decide to go, even though you've been wanting to save money— and afterwards you feel extremely anxious and even angry about spending it, feeling like your friends sabotage you at every turn. You can bet that all of this stress affects your health too.

How does your relationship with money affect your life? Surely, you have your own unique examples. Ask yourself this: *when was the last time you had an argument or awkward moment with someone about money? And what about the last time you had anxiety over a bill?* If you're like most people, your answer to either of these examples is likely *this week, yesterday, or five minutes ago.*

A better relationship with money is the gateway to the life you want, whether that life is filled with luxury vacations, or the ability to become a homeowner, to open your own small business, or simply get out of debt. The essence of my coaching, and what I'm going to teach you, is this: financially secure people have control of their money, and the amount they have is much less important than how they use it and how they feel about it.

When I talk to parents about something I call Money Parenting™, I talk with them about how great it would feel having raised RICH kids. To me, that stands for Responsible, In Control & Happy. Your kids' money habits aren't being taught in school, and they really are learning about money from YOU. This is why I'm starting with YOU! And this is also why mastering your money can help way more than just you, your money and even your honey! It will affect your kids as well as every other area of your life.

What "Financially Secure" Means— And Why So Few People Are

Financially secure people feel just that—secure financially. It doesn't just mean that they have enough money. It's means they are calm and relaxed about money, no matter how much or little they have, because they know where they stand with money, where they want to be ultimately, and what map they are using to get there. They feel in control, positive, and hopeful about their money—not from a place of delusion but out of a deep sense of clarity. They know what their money goals are, and that gives them a sense of direction and purpose. Sound totally alien to you? Don't worry; these people are admittedly the minority.

As a sought after money coach and wealth strategist, I work with individuals to master their finances and help couples prevent money problems from wreaking havoc on their marriages. Having coached and advised thousands of people, I have clients from all fields and professional backgrounds—smart, successful, responsible men and women with careers many people would envy—whose baggage around money has kept them blind to their own habits and choices, locked in vicious cycles for years. That's why they come to me.

People who hire me that get the best results typically feel that they are...

1. Controlled by their money, which limits their choices
2. Frustrated that they can't seem to get ahead
3. Missing opportunities to maximize their wealth
4. Lacking confidence in their financial future
5. Without direction or a strategic financial plan

Regardless of whether your bank account is in the negative or you've got a ton saved up, my message is the same: If money is a major source of stress in your life, facing your limiting beliefs and behaviors is the key to overcoming your money issues.

Let's face it. Money is a very emotional issue. And issues don't go away when you ignore them or try to cover them up.

According to a recent study released on February 4th, 2015, called "Stress in America. Paying with Our Health" money is a top stressor for most Americans. The study notes: "This year's [2015] Stress in America™ survey shows that stress about money and finances is prevalent nationwide. In fact, regardless of the economic climate, money has consistently topped Americans' list of stressors since the first Stress in America™ survey in 2007."

You may have also heard that money is not just causing stress—it's ruining marriages too. As the Huffington Post put it in May 2012, "No. 1 reason marriages end in divorce: money problems."

Unfortunately, money is one of those taboo subjects we're just "not supposed to talk about" in our culture. We're taught that it's rude to ask money questions, even of those closest to us. Heaven forbid you talk about religion, politics or money. But how are we to gauge our relationship with our money if we don't talk about it with those we trust? We talk to friends and family about our boyfriends and girlfriends, so why not money?

Well, there are several answers to this. You can talk to a friend about relationship issues, and your friend will likely not assume that you want them to start making love to you. But bring up money issues, and they might start wondering if you're asking for a loan. And there is also the fear of the rumor mill, right? If you start opening up about your money situation, good or bad, word might get around, and suddenly everyone treats you differently, thinks less of you and your social status.

Most of this is in your head, of course, but not all of it. It's a paradigm that needs to shift in our culture, and your fears about discussing money must be overcome if you're going to have any shot at a strong, healthy relationship with it. With so many people in real money trouble—a depressed economy, crippling credit card debt, student loans and mortgages up the wazoo—let's face it, we need to start talking.

Money and Freedom:
It's Not Just About How Much You Have

It's actually not the fact that you don't have enough money that holds you back from having more choices. What's holding you back is your lack of clarity around money and disempowering feelings about money every day. It's not about how much you have—it's about how you feel about what you have, and whether your money is going towards the things you value and desire the most in life—and if not, whether you have a game plan to make that happen.

If you're barely making ends meet and the act of looking at your money gives you extreme anxiety, you will stay in that pattern indefinitely unless you begin facing the numbers—even if it's uncomfortable initially. On the flipside, you can bring in a million dollars a year, but if you're spending it on every shiny object that crosses your path, you won't be financially secure.

And even if you save half of it but you feel fearful every day about losing it, you're not truly wealthy. You may have money in the bank, but you may be "broke" emotionally—and let's remember that money itself is just paper; it's what money represents that gives it power.

The 10 steps outlined in this book will show you how your feelings are influencing your behavior and determining your current financial reality. It will get you clear on how much you make, spend, and keep each month. It will help you determine your money goals—to boost your income, to work less so you can have more time for leisure or personal goals, to save more, or to feel less anxiety about money—and give you a map to get there.

Once you've established empowering money habits where you continue to keep more each month, you'll be in a position to make money work for you. Most likely, right now you trade time for money. You go to work, or run a business and get paid. Until you have control of your money and are managing it well on a day-to-day basis, making money work for you may seem like a pipe dream. However, once positive money habits kick in (which can happen very quickly, by the way), then you will begin to shift your beliefs and behaviors with money so that you keep more at the end of the month and save. This savings begins to compound and once you have money saved, you have the luxury of getting that money to work for you.

Imagine building a big enough nest egg that pays you more than your job, so you never have to work again! This is the type of freedom and security you can expect when you build a new foundation for your finances.

I've written this book because I am passionate about helping you close the gap between the kind of life you're leading now—one where money may be confusing, stressful, or not being used to its potential—and a life where money is a genuine source of power and happiness for you.

Through my work with couples, I also know the profound way in which money impacts intimate relationships. Marital arguments about money are the top predictors of divorce. Of course, money issues in a marriage are often indicative of deeper problems of trust, communication, and honesty, but those problems cannot be addressed if money issues are ignored or belittled. If you are married, you need to face your issues with money in order to have a secure, abundant financial future with your spouse. Talking about money, having an effective system in place and getting on the same page with your partner can not only keep your relationship intact, it will create a relationship that will thrive.

If you'd like to take my Money & Relationship Quiz, "Is Your Relationship in the Red?" go to www.RobynCrane.com/quiz

If you haven't found that special person yet, resolving your own money issues now will set you up for a solid foundation in your next relationship. I once heard Tony Robbins say, "You need to become the person you want to attract." I believe this completely. If you want to attract someone who is responsible with their money, communicates well about money and faces the truth, then you must first do the same. Maybe, just maybe, the "newer" you, the one who has overcome the money issues that have been standing in your way for so long, will attract the person you're meant to be with.

At the end of this book, you will not only have the tools to improve your money situation— you'll also have the tools you need to feel good about your money, regardless of where you currently stand with it. This might sound like hype or a stretch to you, or maybe it just seems a little farfetched. If so, I know exactly how you feel, because I used to feel the same way.

I Used To Worry and Stress About Money All the Time

Before becoming a financial advisor, I was a singer-songwriter. That was my "business," if you can even call it that. Money didn't come easily to me when I was pursuing music, and even once I made the switch to financial planning, I continued to struggle the first couple of years.

Even though I was good at saving, I wasn't necessarily good at making money. (These are two VERY different things.) In fact, I used to worry and stress about money all the time. I was always watching every dollar I spent and I felt guilty and concerned if I bought something I didn't totally value and appreciate. I didn't yet understand how to be in control of my money or emotions, and because of this, I was frozen. I didn't do much; I didn't buy much. Instead of enjoying life to the fullest, I was held back by my fears and uncertainties. And there was no reason for it.

Looking back, knowing what I know now, my fear of not having enough money or of overspending it far outweighed the reality of my money situation. It took a disproportionate and unnecessary toll on my psychological state.

As meager as my earnings were as a singer-songwriter, I was still able to save but I felt nervous on a daily basis, obsessed with spending as little as possible.

I was hesitant and protective of my money, and though I did spend money on some things that I valued in life, anxiety followed me all along the way. I didn't spend a dime without considering the value I'd get in return. Back then, I didn't know that there was a system for my money, and most importantly that I could take control of my money and prevent it from stressing me out.

But I was young. I wasn't taught how to be successful. I didn't know better and I was often scared.

Getting a Coach Changed My Life

Starting the commission-only based job as a financial advisor only made my anxiety worse. I began to accumulate debt for the first time as I paid for exams, licensing, business fees, office space and even gas as I drove from home to home trying to get clients.

What bridged the gap between where I was and where I wanted to be was getting a coach. I hired an incredible money coach, even though paying for a coach at the time was a total stretch financially (to put it lightly). I accumulated even more debt to get his help, but it was worth it!

This choice completely changed my life. My coach, Jeff, helped me in two major ways: One, he helped me get total clarity about my money so that I was in control of it, and two, he taught me how to make more money by providing even more value to my clients. With Jeff's help, I was able to work less, get my clients better and faster results and grow my income to 6 figures.

Jeff taught me how to understand my own patterns better and I quickly started to make powerful shifts. I was able to turn my own financial situation around - and more importantly, I became in control of my emotions about money. I also got crystal clear about my purpose to help others have a better relationship with money, which is why I have written this book.

So this book is for you — if you are at all like I was — in desperate need of an emotional and practical money tune-up.

I hope you use this book as an opportunity to as an opportunity to improve yourself and become the person you know you are meant to be. As you change your money beliefs and behaviors, your money situation will absolutely change. There's no way it can't.

FREE BOOK UPDATES AND VIDEO TRAINING

This book is INTERACTIVE - to get free training videos, access to more resources and updates and upgrades to this book as new versions are released visit:

http://robyncrane.com/bookbonuses

SPECIAL GIFT

This Is A FREE Invitation That Will Change Your Life!
Free Money Mastery Workshop - Online Classes ($497 Value)

Please immediately go to:
http://www.robyncrane.com/freeworkshop and register yourself right away! It's absolutely free and all it takes is an email to register.

I would like to invite you into my home.

What if you had the opportunity to learn the quickest and easiest way to overcome your money issues, get in control of your money, and experience what I like to call: Total Money Mastery? What if you were literally handed the EXACT model that I've used with countless others, and you created results faster than you ever imagined? Well, I've put together a very special series of free trainings for you.

This is a training where I invite you into my home. I will stand directly in front of you, in my living room and teach you personally. I'll even introduce you to a few of my top clients from around the World to help you transform! The information I help you master has taken me my whole life to perfect. You can have it in just a few hours! I want to personally invite you to this free training series I'm doing called "The Money Mastery Workshop." There is absolutely no catch and no credit card required. You can register for it right away with just your email address.

Just go to http://www.robyncrane.com/freeworkshop and you will quickly be on your way to living the quality of life you deserve!

WARNING:

Space in this training is very limited. This event is 100% free but only for a limited time. In case you have missed the LIVE training sessions, we are going to make the replays available for a short time.

Whatever you do, don't miss it. Save your free seat now!
http://www.robyncrane.com/freeworkshop

What's it about?

"The Money Mastery Workshop" consists of trainings where I will again walk you through the entire system, but this time you'll get to see me going through it with you! Watch and learn as I interact with you regarding all the ins and outs of how this relates to your life. You'll also get to meet our successful friends and clients that I've worked with, and you'll have an opportunity to ask any questions you may have.

*This is your opportunity to join our community of incredible people who want to raise the bar in their lives. Imagine being surrounded by awesome like-minded people just like you! You can get all of this for free. Even if you missed our LIVE presentations, I am going to make the replays available for a limited time only. The replays are also free and you can watch them at your own pace.

Whatever you do, don't miss it. Claim your free seat now.
http://www.robyncrane.com/freeworkshop

PART I:

WHERE YOU ARE

STEP 1 ~

KNOW YOUR MONEY TYPE

You've had a relationship with money your whole life. It's a very deep connection that was established when you were just a young kid. You witnessed your parents' relationship with money and learned to be like them, or possibly to be very *unlike* them - when it comes to money. Growing up, you developed beliefs and patterns about money, which have shaped the relationship you have with money today.

You also have a dominant money type. Knowing what it is and the patterns you run will help you overcome your issues.

Before I dig into the 5 money types, I just want you to know that I am not categorizing you or putting you in a box. You actually have some characteristics of all these different types, personalities or patterns, just as we all do. There are no judgments here. Just have fun figuring out which one of these money types, or which combination of them best represents you and your money beliefs and behaviors.

Also, you may notice that I'm using dolls to represent the different money types. I use these as props in my live seminars to make it fun and easy to understand (for me and you - yes, I know, I'm a dork! ☺)

Disclaimer: These are not my dolls.

They're my husband's.

Just kidding. I've borrowed these dolls from my daughter to best illustrate the money types in my seminars, and I added the pictures here to make it easy to understand and to remind you to take this lightly. (Actually, I more accurately should say that I've "stolen" the dolls from my daughter, since now they're in my possession and she needs to check them out like a library book in order to play with them).

Use the types to help you recognize patterns you run with money. They're just that, patterns. It's not who you are, nor is it something you're stuck with. The money types will help you recognize beliefs and behaviors that may be holding you back from getting what you want.

Here you will be able to identify the character(s) you are most like. Then you'll be well on your way to knowing what and how you want to change.

FIVE MONEY TYPES

<u>Spendthrift Sally</u>

Representing the first money type is a glamorous doll named "Spendthrift Sally," chosen because of her beautiful gown and glittery bling.

Spendthrift Sally tends to spend a lot of money and is an impulsive buyer. She loves to shop and buy nice things. Shopping sprees are commonplace and she justifies her purchases by taking advantage of sales or buying things she *supposedly* needs.

Spendthrift Sally consciously (or unconsciously) is concerned that if she doesn't buy now, she will miss out. She generally feels good when she buys something. It makes her feel comfortable... *initially*.

Some Spendthrift Sallys, especially those who spend more than they make, feel guilty or anxious when reality hits. They get worried or have remorse when the bills come and they can't pay

---

them off or even pay them down. And it happens at times, that a Spendthrift Sally may even behave like a child at times, afraid that her husband is going to get mad at her and give her the cold shoulder, because she spent too much again—behind his back.

Let me give you a real-life example. One of my clients—we'll call her Brenda—is the epitome of a Spendthrift Sally. Brenda is a stay-at-home mom whose husband makes $450,000 a year. Brenda easily spends $2,000 a month on clothes for herself and especially things for her kids. She goes to high-end stores, telling herself they have the money, they deserve nicer things, she needs these things, and the kids definitely need these things. She searches for deals—that is, should she find deals in these nicer stores, the decision is more or less made up for her to take advantage of the discount, even if she doesn't particularly need the thing that's on sale. She doesn't want to miss out.

Many times, Brenda will buy things with every intention of returning them. "I'll see if I like it," she says to herself. Or, "I'll buy a bunch of things and be sure to return half of them." It's just another way she justifies swiping her credit card yet another time.

And she may even end up returning a few items, but nowhere near what she had promised herself initially. And what's more, when she goes back to Neiman Marcus or Bloomingdales to return the few things she's decided she doesn't want, she finds a whole new set of things she does want. She didn't know she wanted it, but she wants it now and *needs* it now. So she buys items, returns them only to buy more items, then goes back to return a few things and once again buys some more. I call this "revolving door shopping." Buy, return and buy more, return and buy more, and on and on.

What does all of this lead to? You can probably guess. Guilt. Anxiety. Lack of control. Fights with her husband. Feelings of remorse. Feelings that are the exact opposite of what Brenda felt in the actual moment of spending money. Making her purchases, she feels secure, she feels in control. She feels she's making her and her family's life better, that their money situation is fine, that they will be better off because of these purchases than they were before—and hey, she even found a deal or two, so she justifies that she's actually saving money!

Only later does she realize that those fleeting sensations of wealth and security and control were only illusions. That whatever void or need those purchases were meant to fill is still there. And when she feels this way, the only thing she wants is to feel that high again, that imaginary sense that all is well and right with the world, and so she shops again.

This is Spendthrift Sally.

Now, if you're a man you might be thinking, "Whoa, I spend a lot of money, but I am not a chick."

Let me be clear. This isn't gender specific. I'm just using silly examples to represent each money type so you can understand to what degree you are like these characters. I've had plenty of male Spendthrift "Sals" on my client list. Instead of catching up on the latest clothing line or buying the nicest jewelry, you may tend to buy the newest electronics - TV, Smartphone, iPad, luxury watch, etc.

A Spendthrift Sally at a 10 (male or female) buys compulsively and impulsively. Maybe you're more of an online shopper. You get click happy on ebay or Amazon. Or maybe every time you fly, you can't resist buying the coolest, latest, newest gadget on Skymall.

Now, I want you to rate yourself, to give yourself an idea of where you stand. Don't do this "later" or two weeks from now when you think, "Now, I am ready to get my money in order."
Do it now. It's simple.

I'll use myself as an example here. Personally, I would rate myself a 3. I actually don't like to spend a lot of money. I like to hoard and save it. I get anxious if I spend too much money, especially impulsively. It's just not my thing. I actually hate to shop. I get overwhelmed by the decision-making. However, in certain circumstances, I do buy impulsively like Spendthrift Sally. I have a weakness for buying seminars and programs, 1) because they usually offer a discounted price and I don't want to miss out and 2) I'm addicted to getting help creating fast results in my life and business. So, I give myself a 3 in this area, because I do actually spend money impulsively from time to time, in areas that I believe will improve the quality of my life.

Good or bad, *everybody* has all these parts. It's just by how much and to what degree. Make sense? I hope so.

Action Step

Put a check mark next to all that apply to help you better rate yourself:

___I spend impulsively
___I love to shop
___I feel good when I'm spending money
___I spend frivolously
___I spend without considering the consequences
___I have credit card debt
___I like having material things (especially the newest things)
___I have guilt or remorse after I've spent a lot of money
___Often times, if I don't buy when there's a discount, I feel like I'm missing out
___I believe there will always be more money

On a scale of a 1-10, 10 being "I am totally Spendthrift Sally" and 1 being "I don't spend money at all", write down your number.

My Spendthrift Sally (Sal) Rating is: _____

Cheap Chip

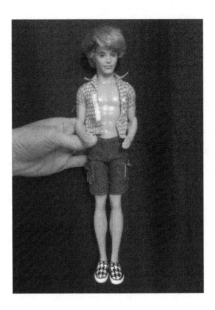

Our second money type is represented by a handsome young man named, "Cheap Chip."

Cheap Chip may look good, but he has been wearing the same outfit for days, weeks or even months. In fact, he's not wearing his shirt unbuttoned like that to be sexy. It just doesn't fit him anymore and he didn't want to spend money on more clothes. He doesn't have much variety either, because he doesn't really like to spend money on himself.

Typically, Cheap Chip doesn't even like to spend money on others. He likes to keep his money close to him. He saves it, even hoards it. He usually has a secret stash somewhere. When he does spend money, he often feels worried and anxious. He definitely doesn't like to "throw money away" on things he doesn't really value.

Cheap Chip considers value when making buying decisions. He may do a lot of research before making a purchase and is always looking for the best deal. He's known for trying to save a buck and some may refer to him as a penny pincher. He would refer to himself as frugal (which is probably accurate and something he is proud of), though some would call him cheap (which he finds insulting). He definitely doesn't like to pay for more than his share and is well aware of what he owes.

For example, at a restaurant with friends, Cheap Chip would likely know exactly how much his share of dinner cost, including tax and tip. (Spendthrift Sally, on the other hand, would be clueless and suggest that they just split the bill, not to be unfair, but because she wouldn't even consider spending money an issue.)

As I just alluded to, I am more like Cheap Chip. On a scale of a 1-10, I actually *used to be* a 10. But, once I understood and implemented the strategies I'm sharing with you in this book, I went through many changes to improve myself. Fact is, Cheap Chip tends to be scarcity minded. When I realized this, and that I wanted more *abundance* in my life, I made changes. Being a fanatical Cheap Chip had its consequences.

I carried around a lot of worry and anxiety when dealing with or thinking about money, and that was based on my fear that I would never have enough. So I embraced abundance by having more faith in myself - I chose to believe I could always make more money and I'd never run out of resources. And I stopped freaking out about every dollar I was spending. I left anxiety at the door. I even offered to pay more when having dinner with friends, instead of making sure I paid only my share.

Nonetheless, of the five money types, today, I'm still most like Cheap Chip –and that's okay. I'll always be a saver at heart, and why shouldn't I be? It has served me well. I even like to "hoard" money a bit. But I no longer have a "secret" stash. My husband knows all about my mounds of silver.

I'm proud to tell you that according to my current self-rating-system, I have given myself a 7 out of 10 as being like "Cheap Chip."

That's progress! And, since I believe progress equals success, I'm going to quickly celebrate my success. (Oh yeah! Feel free to imagine me doing the "cabbage patch" right now. You know the dorky, old school 80s hip-hop dance move? If you don't know it, Google it, it will give you a good laugh!) Ok, moving on.

Action Step

Put a check mark next to all that apply to help you better rate yourself:

___I don't like to spend a lot of money
___I feel good when I save money and believe it's important
___I hoard money (or have a secret stash)
___I'm frugal
___I consider value when making buying decisions
___I love discounts and good deals
___I get anxious or worried when I spend too much money
___I don't like to pay for more than my share
___I don't care very much about having material things
___I believe I may never have enough

Go ahead and rate yourself:

My Cheap Chip (or Chelsea) Rating is: _____

Overgenerous Olivia

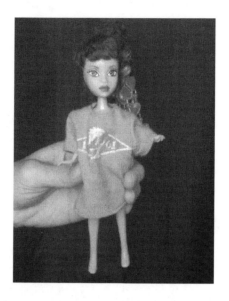

Next, I'd like to introduce you to "Overgenerous Olivia."

You can see that Overgenerous Olivia is in an over-sized T-shirt. She's represented here as someone who tends to wear hand-me downs or homemade clothes. But it's not because she's cheap. This outfit simply demonstrates the idea that sometimes she is so generous, that she doesn't have any money left over to take care of herself. For example, if you're like Overgenerous Olivia, you may buy your nephews iPhones for Christmas, but you're wearing a sweater with holes in it.

Overgenerous Olivia gives and gives and gives…and then gives some more. She is overgenerous and it's often at her own expense. She doesn't focus much on what she doesn't have, she focuses on others and assumes she'll be fine.

It's typical for Overgenerous Olivia to insist on treating her friends for lunch, even though she may make and have less than them. She might say, "You can get me next time," but next time she offers to treat again. Or maybe when out to eat with a bunch of friends, she orders extra appetizers for the group saying that she'll pay for it.

Overgenerous Olivia gives because it makes her feel good and she likes to be thought of as generous and thoughtful. She loves to buy gifts for people and may do this (unconsciously) to get love or buy friendship.

If you're like Overgenerous Olivia, you probably give a generous amount of your income to charities. Sometimes, you'll empty your bank account to give to charities and others first, instead of saving for yourself.

Ironically, as a fervent giver, Overgenerous Olivia may be a horrible receiver. She's been known to refuse help from others or take on so much herself that others assume she doesn't want their help.

She also thinks that other people deserve to have more than she does (though not necessarily consciously).

It is great to be generous, but when you have little left over for yourself, or you're doing it for attention or love, you can get hurt.

Some Overgenerous Olivias give based on their own sense of spirituality, telling themselves it's more virtuous to give to others and unnecessary to be wealthy.

On my TV Show, _The Financial G-Spot_, I once had an Overgenerous Olivia make an appearance—Sarah Jane, we'll call her. At 64 years old, she had 5 different miscellaneous jobs and $10,000 to her name. She came to me for financial advice on whether or not she should invest in a TV show project that she believed would help the elderly. She was ready to commit $5,000 of her personal money (half of her life savings) and had no idea how this TV show would make any money. But she believed in it and she was passionate about helping others with little regard to how it would negatively affect her.

The reason she was in this financial blunder in the first place was because she spent a lifetime of giving her money (and time) away to others who she justified needed it or deserved it more. She'd led a fascinating life, from one job, one experience, to the next, and loved her identity of being extremely generous and thoughtful, but when it came to her own money, she had stress, anxiety and fear buried deep.

In speaking with Sarah Jane—as enthusiastic and wonderful as she is—it became clear to me that she was completely oblivious as to how dire her situations was. And furthermore, the more she talked, the more I could see that Sarah Jane had no real concept of money whatsoever. She simply didn't value it. She assumed money matters would work themselves out: when she needed it, it would come to her; when others needed it, she would offer it. Which might be admirable in an altruistic sense. But in the real world, it meant trouble for Sarah Jane.

Sarah Jane, wanting to help people so much, was so overgenerous that she was willing to put half of her very meager savings into the project. "If" the project ever took off… sure, it would be great for the elderly people she wanted to help —but there are many factors against Sarah Jane's likelihood of success —she didn't have any experience doing this kind of thing before, she didn't have a business plan or business savvy partners to help her, nor did she have much of a clue as to how she could monetize the venture. Great for others, in theory. Bad for Sarah Jane in reality.

I am not much like Overgenerous Olivia. I do like to treat my friends and buy the table an appetizer here and there, but I've made a conscious effort to do so, compensating for my lack of generosity as a Cheap Chip. I typically am not *over* generous. I'm terrible at buying gifts (my husband will sadly agree to that) and I conscientiously give a certain percentage of my income to charity, but not at the risk of hurting my own financial situation. I also work creatively with my family where we get together and do something as a family to give back. However, it has more to do with my beliefs of the importance of giving back than to be acknowledged by others for being generous.

I give myself a 4 for Overgenerous Olivia, because I feel good when I give and have worked on becoming more generous, but I am not overly generous—especially to my own detriment. I have a healthy level of Overgenerous Olivia in me.

Action Step

Put a check mark next to all that apply to help you better rate yourself:

___I love to give to others
___I'm known for being an amazing gift giver
___I give to others with little regard to how it will affect my financial situation.
___I often treat people/pay for them
___I spend more on others than I do on myself
___I like to give to charity, even if it means I have nothing left over to save for myself
___I like that people think of me as a generous and thoughtful person
___I don't feel like I really need or deserve money
___When buying gifts, I'm not very concerned about the cost
___I believe that money will come to me

So rate yourself on a scale of 1 - 10, how similar are you to Overgenerous Olivia?

My Overgenerous Olivia (Oliver) Rating is: _____

Delusional Dan

I'd like to introduce two characters to represent "Delusional Dan." I'm using my daughter's "Super Hunk Doll" together with a short geeky guy to represent this money type.

Delusional Dan thinks he looks like a "Super Hunk," but in reality, he looks more like a short nerdy dude. Sure, he is cute, sweet, and super smart, but he is a little bit *delusional*.

If you are like Delusional Dan, you probably have a nice, beautiful, showy car, or you have a nice house, or you wear nice clothes and you like to show them off. Because being flashy and looking good makes you feel significant. You act like you have a ton, and then you buy more stuff to make you look (and feel) really important.

Delusional Dan typically pretends to be someone he is not. He puts up a good front and thinks he's fooling people. But most can see through Delusional Dan's ways, and have an inkling that behind the luxury watches, cars, and clothes, he's barely getting by or perhaps in deep doodoo.

Another aspect of Delusional Dan is his tendency to jump at opportunities. He doesn't take the time to research good deals like Cheap Chip would, so he fills in the gaps with hope and desire. When he makes money decisions, he does what he wants and hopes for the best, and may also be a bit of a dreamer. He may have pie in the sky goals, but does little to pursue them, having the delusion that it will all just somehow work out.

Delusional Dans do have the ability to think well beyond what most people think is possible, and in this way, they have the potential to accomplish incredible feats. Warren Buffett and Donald Trump have characteristics of Delusional Dans, which is startlingly clear if you simply look at what they believe they can do and the goals they have. But the difference between these extremely successful people and most Delusional Dans is action and follow through. You could and should think big, but if you don't have a plan and follow through on it—let's face it, you're just delusional. But if you think big and take the right action, you can be rich.

Another guest on _The Financial G-Spot_ was Jack, who quickly revealed patterns consistent with a Delusional Dan and Avoider Al (who will be introduced next). He was now in his 40s, still struggling from debt and overspending that started in college. When he got his first credit card at the age of 20, he went crazy. He was all about having gadgets, toys, watches and nice clothes. Jack felt cool, he felt significant and admitted that spending money on classy things and eating were both coping mechanisms he used when he was feeling bad about himself.

These behaviors got Jack into a lot of trouble. He gained weight and bought more stuff to make up for his feeling of inadequacy. By his 30s, his consumer debt had surpassed the $25,000 mark and he couldn't even pay his minimums. He went to a credit card counselor and managed to consolidate his debt, but he only lasted 6 months before he was back in bad habits and began missing payments again.

Jack didn't have all the information that you have to identify his money type in the short time we had together. But, all I had to do to make the distinction between Spendthrift Sally and Delusional Dan was to ask him one question: "Did you buy all of the stuff to look successful or because you really like to shop and told yourself that you needed it all?" He quickly responded that he wanted to look successful. It was clear to me that Jack was predominantly a Delusional Dan.

As the show progressed and we talked about Delusional Dans' money patterns, Jack realized the beliefs behind his compulsive shopping for the first time: He never fully believed he was worthy, significant, or important on his own. This is classic Delusional Dan. He lies to himself about the secret key that's finally going to make him worthy. In his mind on some subconscious level, he thinks, *this purchase or object is going to help me get the feeling of significance that I want.* Delusional Dan perpetually lies to himself, convincing himself that by having nice things, he will be perceived as successful. If material objects could really provide feelings of worthiness, he would have had it by now, and on some level, he knew that.

Once Jack recognized his money type and the beliefs and patterns that went along with it, he felt empowered. Before, Jack thought the answer to his problems was credit counseling, or some other outside source; that something (even more knowledge) could fix his problem. But when he recognized his money type and the patterns and consequences he has experienced and will continue to experience if he doesn't change, he got leverage. He was honest about his situation and not proud of it. He compared himself to his friends who had homes, money, success, and he finally faced the truth—if he didn't step up and change, he would continue to have nothing other than a big pile of debt. Watch the trailer with Jack now by clicking here: www.financialgspot.com/jack.

Do you see? Knowing that he had been "delusional," or dishonest with himself, gave him the power to finally see the truth, which gave him the motivation and path to transforming his beliefs, behavior and his life! This is the power of knowing your money type.

By the end of the show, Jack was able to say out loud and believe that he is worthy! He started to get excited and tell me the truth about himself. He said that he knows people like his personality, that he is a great person, and that people love him for who he is—even in spite of the fact that he has debt and a boatload of problems. He left the show feeling excited and confident that he would no longer let these patterns and beliefs control his life. He recognized that he must seek to feel worthy from within, not from without.

How much are you like Delusional Dan?

I rated myself as a 5 for Delusional Dan. You see, admittedly, I am a bit delusional at times. (My husband regularly teases that it's more than sometimes.)

I don't necessarily like to admit it, but I can be kinda gullible and I definitely can get swept up in the idea of exciting possibilities. When I believe something will help me make money, grow money or learn something at warp speed, I'm quick to think it is a "great opportunity"—and sometimes I just GO FOR IT! More than once, I've hurt myself by investing in "opportunities" when I wasn't really being honest with myself about the truth. It's not always appropriate to invest in EVERY opportunity.

Okay. Confession time.

One year, my husband, daughter and I went to Mexico with my parents during Christmas time. Before our arrival, my parents signed us up for a timeshare presentation so we could take advantage of the special promotion. All we had to do was take a tour of the property and attend a mandatory meeting about the timeshare opportunity, and the company would give us 300 bucks cash! Not bad! The Cheap Chip in me thought of all the fun activities we could do without having to dip into our own pockets!

The thought of owning a timeshare didn't appeal to us in the least, so we knew we wouldn't be taking them up on any offer. My parents were proud owners of timeshares, but to us, it just didn't make sense. We liked the freedom of our travels. But, for 300 buckaroos, we would sit through the boring presentation and then get back to our vacay.

Cut to three hours later. There we were, in a room full of people sitting at small tables, each paired up with a salesperson. A beautiful woman had wined and dined us (and we were still not remotely interested). Then she took us on a tour of the luxury property (still not interested). She showed us the sailboat we'd be able to use (not interested), past the pool and Jacuzzi (no interest) and then finally into this room. We were seated at the table and introduced to our token salesperson, the closer. We listened impatiently to his schpiel (still no interest whatsoever). Then he said a few magical phrases. "Investment opportunity." "Guaranteed rentals." "We find the renters for you." "Short sale." "Only $5,000 today and finance to rest." "One-time offer, today only."

Did I mention that we had zero interest in buying a timeshare?! But suddenly, after hours of boredom and disinterest, my husband gave me that look, that investor's gleam. "Guaranteed rentals?" he said. And I got excited too and said, "Let me look at the numbers."

And I did. I took an hour, maybe more. I crunched everything, meticulously, over and over while my husband tended to our daughter, who perhaps from timeshare exhaustion became suddenly ill. "It works out," I told him. "The money makes sense. At these rates, we're looking at positive cash-flow after only six months."

"Okay!" my husband said, convinced. I took the next shift with our daughter as he went in to quickly sign the paperwork before sundown on Christmas Eve. But when he came out of that office, he said, "That didn't feel good."

Sure enough, when we got back to the hotel and did a little research, we discovered that it was a scam. The "guaranteed" rentals were not guaranteed at all. My parents, who happily had two timeshares for the right reason (vacation) said that they had been told that their place would be easy to rent as well, but the few years they didn't use it, they weren't able to rent it out.

My parents felt awful that we were suckered—"We never in a million years thought you'd actually go for it!" (Neither did we!) But they didn't feel as bad as we did. How could we be so gullible? And we're money people, for crying out loud! This is what we do for a living!

Though perhaps a tad embarrassing, I'm telling you this to show you how easily we can all lose our way with money, no matter who we are, what our background is, and how much money we have. It's not bad to have a little delusion. Especially for investors and entrepreneurs, you have to have some faith, you have to take on risk. But when you're having an alarm-sounding Delusional Dan moment, as we were having that Christmas Eve in Punta de Mita, Mexico, it's time to hit the brakes, make a u-turn, and flee.

Thankfully, we were able to get out of our ridiculous timeshare contract, though it did take some legal maneuvering and months of credit card disputes.

Action Step

Put a check mark next to all that apply to help you better rate yourself:

___I buy expensive or luxury things
___I want people to think I'm successful or important
___I like to talk about or show off my expensive stuff
___I jump at opportunities
___I think and dream big

___I think status is important

___I like having material things (especially if it increases my status)

___I want people to think I have more money than I actually do

___I live by the adage, 'fake it 'til you make it'

___I believe that I'll be a millionaire (or super wealthy) someday

Rate yourself right now on a scale of 1 to 10. How much are like Delusional Dan?

My Delusional Dan (Daniela) Rating is: _____

By now, you can start to see how these delineations are not hard and fast. People are complicated and often resemble a variety of money types, at varying degrees. Sarah Jane, who is an Overgenerous Olivia, was off the charts generous, but the likelihood of having any financial success with a TV pilot without understanding the business is more a Delusional Dan kind of move. Plus, being able to fund an ambitious project like that with only $5K of your personal savings and a Kickstarter campaign you know nothing about is also unlikely. I'm not saying that it's not possible, but without making specific plans and taking massive action, it's improbable, and Sarah Jane had little other than an idea.

Jack, though predominantly Delusional Dan, also ranked high on Avoider Al (who you will soon meet) and Spendthrift Sally.

You too are most definitely a combination of all these money types. And if you're having trouble figuring out which one you most closely resemble, don't worry about it. The goal here is to recognize the patterns you are running that are holding you back. You may know immediately that you're most like Spendthrift Sally, or maybe you are a clear combination of Overgenerous Olivia, Delusional Dan and Spendthrift Sally, not to mention showing glaring characteristics of the last money type, Avoider Al.

For now, just notice it. As you continue to read this book, you'll get more and more clear about how this identification will help you make better choices with your money so you can make and/or save more money.

If you haven't done so already, give yourself a score (from 1 to 10) for each of the money types I just shared with you.

Avoider Al

Our fifth and final money type is "Avoider Al," who is represented by a blind boy doll wearing no shirt. (The bare chest has no significance; I just couldn't find the darn shirt!)

"Avoider Al" is "blind" to his money. If you're like this character, you don't look at your money. You don't see what's really going on. You probably get anxious and worried about money, and so you say to yourself *'as long as I don't look at it, as long as I don't pay attention to it, it's not really that bad.'*

One young 27 year old woman—Katie—was deathly afraid at looking at her money. She had debt, and lots of it. Maxed credit cards. Deferred student loans. Loans from her family. Tons of anxiety. She couldn't even look at her bank accounts without having a panic attack. She needed help, and thankfully she took that first step by asking for it. Because she was willing to be open and honest, she could quickly diagnose her money type as Avoider Al. It was obvious.

Katie knew she was in trouble, but had no idea to what degree. She stopped paying her minimums on her credit cards because she just couldn't see it ever going away. She felt like she was in too deep to even make a dent. She was helpless. She had no plan and no hope. So it was just too painful to deal with it at all. She lied to herself, pretending that it didn't affect her and that ignoring her money issues could somehow make the problems go away.

With this much anxiety, panic and fear, you may assume as well that it's just better for Katie to bury her head in the sand. That maybe she was right, looking at her money wouldn't help—especially when she had little income and no new opportunities on her radar.

But when she started working with me, recognizing her money type and doing the most seemingly unnatural thing—looking at her money, instead of ignoring it—is exactly what gave her hope. Only progress could be made from there.

In fact, once Katie got over the initial stress and tension of looking at her bank accounts and debts squarely in the face—while I was there with her, providing encouragement and coaching—she started to experience a relief she hadn't felt in years. She said it was so much better to have a clear picture of her situation—and that, though it was bad, it wasn't as bad as she was picturing in her head. She immediately felt more responsible, grounded, and clear-headed.

Sometimes Avoider Als can get away with being just fine if someone else is taking care of them and making all the financial decisions. My mom is that type of Avoider Al. My mom met my dad right after college, so she never really had to manage money. My dad handled it all and she avoided it. When he tried to get her involved she'd say, "You'll do a much better job at this than I ever could, honey. I trust you. You handle it."

It frustrated my dad that she wasn't involved, but he took care of it all anyway. My mom was lucky that my dad didn't die young or get so frustrated with carrying all the burden that he let go of the responsibility. But if you're like my mom, you're playing Russian Roulette. It's a huge gamble.

Not everyone is as lucky as my mom. I've heard terrible stories of divorce, bankruptcy and even suicide.

I don't want anything like this, to happen to you. I don't want money to ruin your mood, let alone your relationship, or your life. This is the kind of thing that brings me to tears, but also drives me to teach people to face their money issues head on and experience the wonderful relief and genuine happiness it provides. Tough in the beginning, yes, but it pays back in spades.

Avoider Al is the most dangerous and also most frequent money type I see, and it tends to accompany others. Delusional Dans tend to avoid because they've convinced themselves that even though they're not where they want to be now, they will be somehow be there later, so there's no point focusing on what they don't have. Act as if, and avoid reality.

Overgenerous Olivias avoid because it's horrific to think that such an honorable characteristic such as generosity should have any negative consequences. Focus on others, so you don't have to admit the truth about yourself.

Spendthrift Sallys avoid too—those with a spending addiction have an even harder time admitting their difficulties and looking at their finances. Shop your problems (and negative emotions) away.

Even Cheap Chips can avoid.

One of my Cheap Chip clients, Dana, who had always been a saver completely lost track of her money because she and her husband were so different. Her husband was a spender, most dominantly Delusional Dan and Dana felt like she had no control. She was so stressed about money, that she just started to avoid it. She didn't want to talk about it, she didn't want to fight.

And out of fear of just how bad things really were, she began to avoid looking at their money altogether. Even penny-pinchers can become Avoiders.

Like everyone, I avoid things, but I don't avoid money. I've learned that looking at my money, no matter how bad it is, is still less stressful than avoiding it. (And trust me, I've rolled plenty of credit card balances in my day). I'd rate myself a 1 for Avoider Al.

Now rate yourself. How much are you like Avoider Al? 1 to 10?

Note:
Just as these types are not gender specific, I am also not indicating in any way that blind people are blind to their money. I'm just using it as an analogy. (Just to make sure you didn't draw any weird conclusions here.)

Action Step

Put a check mark next to all that apply to help you better rate yourself:

___I don't look at my money
___I feel anxious when thinking about my money
___I am totally unclear about how much money I have or owe
___Someone else deals with my (our) money, so I don't need to be involved
___I can't handle looking at my money

___I don't see many advantages of paying attention to my money

___Money is too stressful to focus on

___I'm just not good with money

___Reading this book is a huge step for me, because I really don't want to deal with my money issues

___I believe that looking at my money will make me feel worse

How much are like Avoider Al? Rate yourself right now on a scale of 1 to 10.

My Avoider Al (Ali) Rating is: _____

Now that you know all the money types, you can identify which character is most dominant for you. Go back and look at your ratings in comparison to the others to double check if the sequence feels accurate.

So, *what are your strongest money types?* Is there more than one? Is there one that you are especially NOT like, where you got a really low number, like I did on Avoider Al?

Remember, there is no right or wrong here. It's just an assessment of where you are now.
The reason it is so important to identify your money type is because it empowers you to change.

Classifying yourself as a type actually separates who you are from the patterns you are running. It seems counter intuitive, but it's true. As you realize that you're a combination of Spendthrift Sally and Avoider Al, for example, you can recognize that you're just exhibiting a series of behaviors, typical of *many* people. Then, you have choices. When you're aware of your tendencies, you're no longer a victim of circumstance or your "situation." You're able to recognize how the steps you're taking every day are creating your financial situation. Then, you can take that power back. For many people, just knowing this inspires change. Isn't it exciting?!

You might be wondering what types wealthy people are. Well, wealthy people have characteristics of all the types as well, to varying degrees—and whether consciously or unconsciously, they've found ways to make their "type" work for them.

A wealthy Spendthrift Sally likely makes a very high income to support her spending habits without guilt or shame, and still have plenty to save and invest. A wealthy Cheap Chip is an extreme saver, very conscientious about every dollar he spends, but still focuses on all that he has. A wealthy Overgenerous Olivia is overly involved in charities and philanthropy, but not at the expense of hurting herself. Wealthy Delusional Dans are wealthy because of the great risks that they take, and ability to believe that anything is possible. But here's the warning about wealthy Avoider Als. Wealthy Avoider Als on their own (meaning they are not riding on the coattails of someone else who makes financial decisions on their behalf) won't be wealthy for very long. You can't hold onto wealth if you avoid your money and bury your head in the sand.

So, you don't have to change your money type or eliminate your natural tendencies to be wealthy. That would probably take a lifetime of therapy for little benefit at all. All you need to do to invite wealth into your life is recognize the patterns that no longer serve you and shift your behaviors.

WARNING:
ONLY identify your *own* money type.

Discovering your money type is something that each person must do for themselves. Be careful not to start categorizing other people (your partner, your parents, your siblings, your friends) into what you think their money types are. Even if you think you know what their primary type is… keep it to yourself. People tend to feel judged when they're being sized up. Trust me, I know.

When I first came up with these money types, I identified my husband's money type and told him about it, thinking it would help him.

It went something like this... "Hi honey, I've been doing some thinking, and I think 'blah, blah, blah... and that means blah, blah, blah..."

Instead Trevor felt judged, upset and hurt, and we got into an argument.

However, when I gave him a chance to figure it out himself, he discovered his type on his own and felt empowered.

Most people don't like to be told what to do, and no one likes to be told who you *think* they really are. No one likes to feel judged.

That goes for YOU, too.
Don't judge yourself harshly either.

Be kind to yourself and use this exercise as motivation, not as an excuse to beat yourself up.

So, rate only yourself. Then, once you know your money type and the tendencies you may have, you can share it with your partner, siblings or friends so they can help support you.

Want a more accurate assessment?

Take the full Money Type Quiz here:
www.RobynCrane.com/moneytypequiz

<u>Money Types And Relationships</u>

As you can imagine, it's not uncommon for your dominant money type to be different than your partner's. Even having similar money patterns, doesn't ensure that you will automatically see eye to eye when it comes to managing your money and making money decisions. So how does knowing your type help you when it comes to relationships?

By identifying with the money types yourself first, it actually allows you see that this is not *who* you are, it's just a series of patterns that you run, some of which serve you and some of which hold you back. Becoming aware of your own tendencies and understanding the patterns of all the money types allows you to be more accepting of not only yourself, but of your partner. Coming to any conversation about money from this standpoint leads to open communication and enables you to appreciate what you and your partner bring to the table.

One of the couples I worked with—Dana and Matt—(who I briefly touched upon earlier) really illustrate how different money types could hurt a relationship if unaddressed. In their case, Dana was the Cheap Chip. She typically would examine every bill. She'd watch every dime. She spent little on herself or going out and having fun. She used to get anxious about spending money and preferred to just save as much as possible, saying things like, "we don't really need that."

As with many relationships, opposites have seemed to attract, because her husband, Matt couldn't have been farther from a Cheap Chip. Matt is a police officer who also owns his own business. Matt was (and is) more like a Delusional Dan. He's the type of guy who's always looking for a big return on his investments, his eyes are wide open for entrepreneurial opportunities, and he's all about the fun stuff that money can buy.

He has the latest technology and even owns an old luxury sports car. He works hard and believes he deserves to have expensive taste and he most definitely thinks BIG.

You're already getting the picture, right? These are not two personality types that traditionally play well together. And that's just what I saw when they came in for their first consultation. They could not understand each other. They could not fathom how the other person dealt with money. And because of this, transparency and communication were low. Dana got tired of fighting and decided she would simply be totally uninvolved in the finances, she began avoiding.

Matt continued to take huge risks, which ultimately resulted in bankruptcy. This sent Dana into a spiral of powerlessness and resentment, mostly keeping quiet but having the occasional blow up where she blamed Matt for acting irresponsibly. This sent Matt into a spiral of defensiveness and doubt. "How can I be with someone so cautious?" "How can I be with someone who doesn't support my dreams?"

You may think these two were hopeless.

But actually, there is absolutely no reason why these types should not get along. Once Dana understood that she was stuck in a Cheap Chip scarcity mentality, and Matt realized his inner Delusional Dan was lacking follow through on his big ideas, the two were motivated and able to make shifts. They both were more accepting of each other and worked on shifting the patterns that were no longer serving them.

As we worked together using my "4 Keys to a Richer Relationship" System, their communication improved and they transitioned to total financial transparency with one another. Instead of going head to head, Dana could provide a conscientious balance to Matt's opportunism.

At first, Dana and Matt weren't even aware that they were exhibiting these types. Once they were identified, the couple worked on their own money issues individually and that alone improved their communication and their relationship. (Again, as I just mentioned above, the free guide to the "4 Keys to a Richer Relationship" can be found at www.RicherRelationship.com). Remember, when it comes to identifying money types, self-diagnosis is key.

Knowing your money types gives you more power. For now, your only job is to know yours. Whatever your money type, recognize that your patterns are serving you in some way. This awareness gives you the power of choice. You now get to pick and choose what you'd like to get rid of and what you'd like to keep. In the next steps, you will learn the specific actions you can take to begin to get your money in order. Most importantly, you will be able to understand why having clarity about your money can transform your life. As you progress through the book, you will read example after example to help inspire you to take new action in your life, which will pave the path for a new financial future.

Until then, here are some quick tips to get you moving in the right direction. Remember, your money types don't have to control you. Knowing your type gives you the power to make new choices.

Take the full Money Type Quiz here:
www.RobynCrane.com/moneytypequiz

Quick Tips For Each Money Type

If you want to buy something, *Spendthrift Sally*, wait a day. Then if you still want to buy it tomorrow, go ahead. Start by simply pausing before an impulsive buy and asking yourself, "How will I feel when I get the bill for this? Do I really need to buy this, or am I just trying to feel good in the moment?"

Cheap Chip, separate out a certain amount of money each month to just blow on anything. Maybe it's $100 or maybe just $10. Just commit to an amount and force yourself to spend it frivolously every single month. It's a great way to practice abundance.

Give more to yourself, *Overgenerous Olivia*. Do something to treat yourself or buy something you've had your eye on. Or, at a minimum, say "no" every once in awhile. You don't always have to be the one to sacrifice your time or money for others.

Delusional Dan, keep dreaming, but make sure to take action too. Look at one of your big goals and take one action today towards that goal. This could be something as simple as making a phone call or researching for 15 minutes. And the next time you feel compelled to buy something, ask yourself, "Do I want this for myself or so others see me in a certain light?"

And *Avoider Al*, start looking at your money. Do a quick review of how much money you have by looking at your bank statement, for starters. Trust me, that even though it may be painful at first to have clarity of exactly where you are, very quickly you will see the value of knowing the numbers and getting more in control. However bad it is, it can always get better.

<blockquote>

No matter what your money type,
you have the power to shift your behaviors
and start feeling good about money.

</blockquote>

Action Step:

My Top 2 Dominant Money Types Are:

PRIMARY: _____

SECONDARY: _____

If your partner has gone through this exercise (on their own) fill this in. (Good info to know!)

My Partner's Top 2 Dominant Money Types Are:

PRIMARY: _____

SECONDARY: _____

HAVING FUN YET?

This book is INTERACTIVE - to get free training videos, access to more resources and updates and upgrades to this book as new versions are released visit:

http://robyncrane.com/bookbonuses

STEP 2 ~

UNCOVERING YOUR MONEY MaSK™

In order to have mastery of your money, you have to pay attention to it. And getting clarity about how much you "Make, Spend & Keep" is the easiest and best way to start. I call this your Money MaSK™.

As you probably know, every time you talk to your friends and neighbors, you are wearing some sort of *mask*. You are representing yourself by the things you say, the way you act, the clothes you wear, the stuff you buy and so on. People *think* they know who you are. They *think* they know your situation and may even assume you make or have a certain amount of money. Though they often times have no idea what the truth is, it doesn't really matter. Because people form snap judgments all the time. That's how we all survive.

We all wear masks. It can be kind of fun and exciting when you go out and meet other people to be whoever you want to be.

But here's the thing. This is VERY important. When you look in the <u>mirror</u>, you <u>cannot</u> wear a mask. This is the time you need to take it off and be honest and authentic about *who you are*, *where you are*, and *what's going on*.

Like most people, you are wearing a mask, even in front of the mirror.

You are probably not always *totally* honest with *yourself* about your financial situation. Even if your situation is good rather than bad, when you're wearing a mask, you aren't being clear about your money and you can get hurt.

Here's a simple example: if you're not clear on how much money you have in your bank account, you may overdraft and that does you no good! You may say, *"that doesn't hurt, it's no big deal."* When your money takes a hit, your life takes a hit. You take choices out of the equation. You allow money to control you and then the stress creeps in.

And if you are lying to yourself about your money, telling yourself, *"it'll just work out,"* while you do nothing to change the things that aren't working, here's what will likely happen: Cut to when you're 64 like Sarah Jane, and you'll still be singing the same song.

It will just work out, but you have to make it work out!

Clarity About Your Money
Will Give You More Choices

You must get very clear about your money. As I said earlier, money is the gateway to having more choices in your life.

As you may have noticed, "Money MaSK™" has a double meaning here. Uncovering your Money MaSK™ has to do with removing your false mask so that you no longer lie to yourself about your money situation. It also stands for how much you Make, Spend, and Keep. This means gaining total clarity about every dollar that comes in, goes out, and is saved at the end of each month.

Included at the end of this chapter is a very simple spreadsheet you can use to uncover your Money MaSK™. Many people get all worked up about this part, but this document makes it really simple to write down and keep track of how much you Make, how much you Spend and how much you Keep.

Estimate your Money MaSK™

For now, estimate what your Money MaSK™ is. At the end of the chapter you will use a worksheet to get more accurate. Ultimately, you need to be very specific and write down the exact numbers. But for now, take baby steps. Do the best you can. Make your best guess, so you can compare it to the facts later. It will be interesting for you to see how close you are to the truth.

Over time, you will be paying attention to this throughout the month and it will get easier to track. For this exercise, you just need a rough idea to begin the process of having total clarity about your money.

Action Step:

Fill in the blanks. (Estimate without looking at anything else.)

Today's date is: _____

The estimated amount I (or we) MAKE each month is
$_____

The estimated amount I (or we) SPEND is $_____

Income (MAKE) $_____ minus expenses (SPEND) $_____
= $_____ save (KEEP)

If you're in a committed relationship, do this exercise together. Even if you have separate accounts, look at your money as a big picture. You're in this for the long term and your money affects your future together, so you must have transparency about the finances. Start with your Money MaSK™.

Remember, when you gain *clarity* you have more *choices*.
Choices = Freedom!

Right now, your bills come, and you pay them—or you don't. A month later, there they are again, staring you in the face. You don't even think about it. You write that check, or maybe it automatically comes out of your bank account. The bills just come. You either can pay them off or you can't. It doesn't feel like you have much choice, right?

Well, when you look at your Money MaSK™ and divide up your expenses into categories, you'll be able to see where *specifically* you're spending money. Then, as you can gain control of your money, new options will begin to emerge. If you're not making enough to cover your expenses and put money toward your goals, you either decide to spend less or make more. You can absolutely find ways to do both. The point here is shifting your behavior to improve your money.

Spend Money On What You Really Value

One of my young clients, Hannah (an Avoider Al/Cheap Chip), really wanted to go attend regular Yoga classes. The package offered at her local yoga studio cost $80 a month, which was a tough expense to justify, so Hannah assumed yoga was simply a luxury she "couldn't afford." But after doing her Money MaSK™, Hannah got clear about where her money was going and how much was left at the end of the month. She was right, there wasn't much left for yoga. But something interesting happened once she saw the exact amount she had left over: she got motivated to figure out how she could make this work, because yoga was important to her.

With this in mind, she started searching for other options. She knew she could cut expenses a little somewhere, but $80 was a stretch. With just a little bit of research, Hannah soon found a yoga class online for only $18 a month. She decided she'd rather pack a lunch more often instead of eating out, and pocket the extra money for her classes. She was stoked! In the past, she would have assumed yoga wasn't an option for her.

Before, Hannah's money was controlling her. But by looking closely at her expenses, she was able to cut back slightly on something else in order to fit in something new that she valued even more.

The truth is, it's not about whether or not you can "afford" something—it's all about making choices.

I've seen it time and time again with my private clients. When they actually keep *meticulous* track of their Money MaSK™, they tend to have more money at the end of the month! Imagine that! Most people find more "month" at the end of their money! (meaning they've spent all the money they made that month well before the end of the month).

It is truly amazing. Now, I am NOT saying it is just going to happen without you doing anything. Nope, that won't work. However, I have seen some INCREDIBLE results when my clients start paying close attention to their money, like unexpected tax refunds or a boom in their business. I even had a client who increased her net worth in one day by $30,000...and she had NO ASSETS. (if you're dying to know what happened, don't worry. I give all the details in Step 3.)

When you have clarity, <u>you</u> get to choose where your money goes!

Maybe you spend a lot of money on clothes, *Spendthrift Sally*—but in the end you don't even value everything you bought. If you bought 5-10 dresses per month, becoming aware of how much you value your purchases after some time has passed will help you reconsider your behavior. You may think, *"If I just buy the one or two that I really love, I can still feel good and be happy, especially if I knock down some of that credit card debt."*

Or maybe you'll notice that there's something you're spending money on that you don't even care about. You can cut that out and spend it on something else, or save your money for one of your bigger, and more important, future goals.

Remember Katie? Poor anxiety-ridden Katie, hoping her finances would just disappear if she didn't look at them? Well, not only did her debt fail to disappear (in fact, it was getting steadily worse), but the longer Katie avoided the problem, the more she panicked. She was literally being haunted by her own spending, and she wasn't even a huge spender!

It wasn't easy for her, but once we sat her down to fill out her Money MaSK™, she felt immediately better. The situation wasn't great, but it was totally salvageable (it's always salvageable). When you avoid that long hard look in the mirror, like Katie did, those financial demons have all the power. They lurk in the darkness, and you imagine all the horror they might inflict, even though you pretend that they don't exist. But once you shine light on them, no matter how bad they are, they are never as monstrous as your imagination painted them to be. Those numbers become real, and with real numbers, you can begin to come up with a plan to make it better.

With Katie, we looked at her money together and realized that she was right, she didn't have enough. Specifically, she didn't have enough money to pay the bills that month and her minimum credit card payment of $250 was due that day (I know, what are the odds?). Her only plan was to avoid her money because addressing the issue was just too painful. This meant, had we not intercepted this "brilliant plan," she would have missed her credit card payment and been charged a $25 penalty in addition to all the interest that was piling up. But she didn't have enough money in her account, and no paycheck was coming in. So what did we do?

We got crystal clear on every bill she had to pay by what date. We discovered how short she was and by what date she needed more money in her account. The clock was ticking. She had one week.

You want to know what my advice was? I ask her if it was an option for her to borrow the money from her parents. At 27, that scenario sounded like death, but as awful as that option was, Katie said they would likely be able to help. She then felt empowered because she had a <u>choice</u>: Miss her payments and owe even more money, or bite the bullet and ask for a favor.

I'm not suggesting that you borrow money to solve your problems.

The point is, once you have clarity, you have choices. You can change unwanted patterns, like limiting (or eliminating) debt or overspending.

In Katie's case, she valued building a good credit score, one day being debt free, and the satisfaction of knowing she can be trusted to pay back what she owes. And ultimately, she wanted to make money work for her. She didn't value some of the mindless purchases she made regularly, nor did she value the feeling of being constantly broke.

When you begin to notice what you value and what you don't, you get to choose your own adventure! You'll begin to make smarter money choices. You'll start to develop a solid foundation of positive money management skills, so you can reach any of your money goals!

Complete your Money MaSK™ today.

Don't try to do it perfectly at first, but get as accurate as possible. Use your bank account and credit card statements to help you get close. If you spend a lot of cash, you'll have to estimate this time around. But next time, keep a tally sheet, so you can get a clearer and clearer picture.

If this makes you nervous, or anxious, just take a deep breath. Many people experience anxiety when talking about their money. You're not alone.

But the anxiety will start to dissipate the more you look at your Money MaSK™. Trust me. Just take your time, do little by little if you have to, but do not avoid this. It's very simple. It's very important.

Action Step:

Fill out the Money MaSK™ worksheet now.
(Go to www.RobynCrane.com/templates to get the worksheet.)

You can do it!

When you're done, write down the totals in each of the three areas. Fill in the blanks below and compare them to the Money MaSK™ you wrote down earlier.

Today's date is: _____

The actual amount I (or we) MAKE each month is $_____

The actual amount I (or we) SPEND is $_____

Income (MAKE) $_____ minus expenses (SPEND) $_____ = $_____ save (KEEP)

How close was your first guess to the truth?
Did you guess it was worse than it is or better than it is?
What, if anything was surprising to you?

Download the Money MaSK template at
www.RobynCrane.com/templates

THIS IS AN INTERACTIVE BOOK WITH FREE VIDEOS!

Please register to get free training videos,
access to more resources and updates and upgrades to this
book as new versions are released visit:

http://robyncrane.com/bookbonuses

STEP 3 ~

TRACK YOUR NET WORTH

Net worth, oh my gosh. I said it… The dreaded words "net worth."

I know it is a money term, but stay with me. I'm going to make it super-simple for you. Picture a balloon. Imagine that you filled that balloon with some air. Maybe a little, or maybe a lot, but fill it as much or as little as you like. Now tell me, *how much air is in it?*

Well, unless you really *measure it* (and I have no idea how to measure air, but I know it's possible) you wouldn't be able to answer my question. Maybe you'd say something vague like, "three breaths."

Now, let's pretend that the balloon you filled was *your* net worth. Do you see how it's hard to describe exactly how big it is? And, let's say you added a little bit more air, say half a breath. Wouldn't it be difficult to really notice when it got a little bigger? Or even smaller? Well, this balloon is just like your money. Without measuring it, you don't know what you have. And if you don't track your net worth on a monthly basis, you'll never know if your net worth is the size of a hot air balloon or maybe more like an old-sad-wrinkly-deflated helium balloon from last year's birthday party.

Wouldn't it be great to know how much your net worth is and whether or not it's growing or shrinking?! Net worth may be a fancy term, but it is really very simple.

Tracking your net worth tells you whether you're getting RICHER or POORER each month.

And looking at your money can yield surprisingly positive results pretty quickly. Here's an incredible example.

I had a young client named Sophia, who was in a lot of debt when we began working together. We met regularly for a few months and set mini-goals to help her get her finances in order and chip away at paying down her debt. Before our first meeting she had very little clarity about where she stood financially. She knew she had a lot of debt and not a lot of income. As she gained a clear picture of her debt and became more comfortable with the reality of her situation, she began talking about it with her friends and family. And then, in one single day, Sophia increased her net worth by $30,000!

Sounds unbelievable, right? Well, here's what actually happened.

Hearing that Sophia was working with a money coach and was totally committed to getting out of debt, her great aunt, who had been a saver her whole life and had a hefty retirement account, took an interest in helping her.

One day, out of the clear blue, her great aunt offered to pay off her student loans. Sophia was blown away and, of course, a bit hesitant to accept this generous gift at first. After a long talk with her aunt and a pep talk from me, she decided to take it. And just like that, Sophia was $30,000 richer! This story is a true testament to what can happen when you start paying attention to your money.

This specific option is probably not available to most people, but the point is that when you have your financial priorities in line, things tend to fall into place. It seems almost magical, but really, it's because you're directing your effort and energy toward your money. You know what your goal is and where your focus should be, and as you put that forth into the world, you allow the right people and opportunities to come to you.

How To Calculate Your Net Worth

To calculate your net worth, all you have to do is subtract how much you OWE (liabilities) from how much you OWN (assets) at the end of the month, or even right now. It's just a quick snapshot.

$$\text{OWN (assets) - OWE (liabilities)} = \text{NET WORTH}$$

If you own your house or your car, for example, you would include the approximate values. Also, you own your checking account, your savings accounts, money markets and CDs. And you own your investments. That is your money. Those are your assets.

You could add your diamonds, or other physical assets (like gold and silver), but just add that stuff if you plan to sell them someday. Don't add in your furniture or other miscellaneous stuff. That's not necessary. You're going to track the value of every asset, so keep it simple.

Once you have the total of your assets, you then subtract what you OWE, or your liabilities. This includes your mortgage and other loans like car debt, student loans, credit cards and any lines of credit. You should add in loans from family and friends as well. Your assets minus your liabilities equals your net worth. If you've done the math, you will now get a number, and that is your net worth.

$$\text{ASSETS - LIABILITIES} = \text{NET WORTH}$$

Action Step:

For now, <u>estimate</u> your net worth so you can compare it at the end of the chapter.

Fill in the blanks.

Today's date is: _____

The estimated value of my assets is $_____

The estimated value of my liabilities is $_____

Assets $_____ minus liabilities $_____ = my estimated net worth $_____.

If you're in a committed relationship, this is important to do with your partner as well. Look at your "joint" net worth. If you want to keep your money separate, at a minimum, be transparent about the numbers.

Most people have no idea what their true net worth is, or can't even venture a good guess.

The fact is, some people *blow it up* (they think their net worth is much bigger than it is, as *Delusional Dan* is likely to), while others *shrink it down* (inaccurately assuming it's smaller than it really is; some Avoider Als may do this). But either way, they aren't actually tracking it.

Train Your Brain

When you look at your net worth <u>accurately</u> and you see that it gets even just a little bigger from one month to the next, it is an incredibly awesome feeling. I'm telling you, money can't buy this feeling.

The idea here, *and a tricky little secret*, is to <u>train</u> your <u>brain</u>. When you see those numbers month-to-month and side-by-side, your brain wants next month's number to go up, not down. When it goes down, and sometimes it will, do NOT judge yourself. Don't beat yourself up! Your job is simply to *notice* that it went down. That in and of itself is progress because you've engaged in a new behavior. And progress equals success, because you are improving! As you shift your beliefs and behaviors, your bank account will start to change. It may not happen overnight, so please trust in the process.

Here's what I mean. Looking at your money in a new way, empowers you to make a change. Even though your money didn't change in that moment, you're telling your brain that you acknowledge you have a problem and so your brain starts to look for ways to solve it. I know, it sounds a little kooky, but your unconscious mind is powerful beyond measure.

It's very important that you continue to track your net worth on a monthly basis. Doing it once helps, but tracking it every month is crucial to your ongoing success.

For example, if you notice your net worth *continue* to go down each month, let's face it, you'll be clear that you need to start changing your behaviors. But again, the good thing is that YOU KNOW what's going on! That is the first step toward changing things. And if you're looking at your Money MaSK™ as well, you'll know what areas to focus on to KEEP more at the end of each month. Maybe you'll be motivated to start a side business and you'll start to <u>MAKE</u> more money. Or maybe you'll be shocked at what you're spending your money on and so you'll start to <u>SPEND</u> less. Or perhaps the problem is not about how much you KEEP.

Maybe your problem is that you're not growing the money you already have.

As you monitor your net worth, you may notice that your investments are going down, so you may choose to change your investment strategies. If you were tracking your net worth in 2008 when the market was crashing, you may have noticed that your money was not working for you. (It actually it was working against you.) With this awareness, you may have shifted to a more conservative investment strategy, or at least gotten a second opinion.

You can choose to do what serves you best, and the point here is that knowing your money GIVES YOU CHOICES.

When you have more choices, you have more power.

Now that you understand its importance, you can start by calculating your net worth.

Gather Your Statements

The best way to get started with this is to begin gathering all your statements: bank accounts, retirement investments, brokerage accounts, credit cards, loans, etc.

Fill In The Spreadsheet

Use the spreadsheet accessible at the end of this chapter and write down the value of each asset and each liability as of the last day of last month. So, if you're reading this on March 15, you would use your values as of February 28.

Do the best you can. If you can't find a statement, or figure out the value of one or two things, just skip it. You can always come back to it later. The goal is to get as clear a picture as possible, but if this is new to you, you may just need to get it good enough. It may be tedious or overwhelming at first to gather all your assets and account and debt information. But once you do get all the paperwork together or access it all online, it's easy. You're just copying one number from one place to another. Download the simple spreadsheet at www.RobynCrane.com/templates and grab a calculator to do the math. Or, if you know how to create your own spreadsheet, you can set it up to calculate for you.

This may be incredibly simple for you, or may be challenging.

If it's hard at first, trust that it will get easier and easier. Before long you'll become much more effective at using this tool to help you grow your net worth.

Remember Dana and Matt? Dana (Cheap Chip/Avoider Al) was stressed and anxious all the time because her husband, Matt (Spendthrift Sally/Delusional Dan), was spending a lot. Well, when they began to track their Money MaSK™ and net worth, things started to shift. Dana felt empowered by having a visual point of reference to quickly understand what was going on with their money.

They had filed a bankruptcy, so initially it seemed silly to them to monitor their piddly net worth. The only assets they had were a few thousand dollars in their checking account, which they weren't sure would even last until next month. But at my urging, they tracked their net worth anyway—and when that number started to go up every month, even though the *amount* didn't change their lives, the way they felt and communicated changed drastically. They felt excited and empowered by their progress and were finally back on the same team again.

With a quick glance at their Money MaSK™, Dana was clear about how much was coming in, going out and specifically where the money was actually going. Most of the expenses (which before she viewed as extravagant) she now agreed were actually necessary. And being aware of which purchases she disagreed with gave her something specific to discuss with her husband, instead of randomly blaming or judging him.

Whether in a relationship or not, tracking your net worth will give you a clear picture of where you are. From there, you get to choose what areas to focus on and what actions to take.

Action Step:

Go ahead and fill out the net worth worksheet now or schedule time on your calendar to do so.

Download it at www.RobynCrane.com/templates.

Watch what happens month to month and you will very likely start making shifts in your life.

CHECK THIS OUT
In one of the free videos I share with you, I'll guide you through some powerful strategies to help you achieve faster results.
Visit:

http://robyncrane.com/bookbonuses

PART II:

WHAT'S HOLDING YOU BACK

STEP 4 ~

FACE YOUR ISSUES

You have issues. It's okay, so do I.

I used to have <u>major</u> money issues. You've already heard about many of them. Recognizing that I rated extremely high as a Cheap Chip allowed me to acknowledge the patterns I was running that weren't serving me.

For example, feeling stress and anxiety about spending money was something that took me years to overcome. And even though I teach this stuff now, I still have some issues lurking in the shadows.

I am still very conscious about spending money and sometimes consumed about how or where to spend it, but because I have faced my issues, (and continue to face new issues as they arise), I no longer feel like money controls me. I can turn my negative emotions around and use any glimmer of money stress or anxiety as motivation to take action. This is the power I'd like to give to you as you continue to read this book.

I want you to be able to get rid of money stress and be in control of your money and your emotions.

It's not that surprising, really, that money is an ever-present problem for people—but it doesn't have to be. Money is something you have to deal with every day, which is why ignoring your money issues just doesn't work. If you don't face your issues and instead keep your problems bottled up inside, it's only a matter of time before you end up broke, miserable or divorced (or God-forbid, all of the above).

When you face them, you can overcome them. That's why you're here, right? So, before you get started, try to mentally detach yourself from your issues. Your issues don't represent who you are. Remember to be gentle with yourself. This is not a time to judge yourself or make yourself wrong. Instead, recognize your issues so that you can feel empowered, *not embarrassed.*

I'll give you an example of how I've helped clients face their issues, so they had the power to overcome them.

Early on in my financial planning career, I started working with a couple in San Francisco, Chelsea and Kevin. At the time, I was a typical financial advisor. I helped them get life insurance, set up and automatically save into their kids' college funds, and I managed Chelsea's IRA. It wasn't until a year or two later, as I worked with other couples to help them get in control of their money and improve their communication about money, that Chelsea and Kevin asked for my help with their relationship.

Until they confided in me, I didn't know the depth of their issues, but I did know that they were both Avoider Als. The 6-inch stack of unopened financial statements in their kitchen was just one big clue.

Chelsea had a solid 6-figure income, working for the state and Kevin ran his own restaurant, making little profit. They, like most middle class Americans, were barely getting by and felt like they had little control over their money or financial situation.

Chelsea and Kevin had no problem discussing financial planning topics, like investing or saving for their retirement, because financial planning is not a taboo subject. Of course, in our culture talking about financial planning is the responsible thing to do. But talking to your financial advisor about your marital problems —

like lack of communication, frequent money arguments and resentment about money—wasn't typical.

It wasn't until their marriage was on the brink of divorce and after they witnessed me help so many others with their money and relationship that they pulled the trigger to work with me in a coaching capacity, to get help with their *real* issues.

Their issues unraveled quickly and the tension skyrocketed in our first coaching session. Chelsea began passive aggressively blaming Kevin for many of their money problems. He hadn't done his taxes in over 5 years, he had no clarity about how much money he was making in his restaurant business, he wasn't contributing enough financially. In that first session, Kevin mostly sat with his arms crossed, defended himself, returned blame and then stormed out towards the door, but luckily never left the room.

This is a typical scenario for people who have avoided their issues for so long. Everything had stacked and stacked to a point where they had so much fear, resentment and blame that they were on the fast track to divorce.

So how did I help them face their issues? We started with one issue at a time.

I used a simple strategy.

1. Isolate each issue.
2. Decide to solve it.
3. Take one action step.

We isolated each issue, decided which to solve and each week, Chelsea and Kevin would take action towards solving the problems.

For example, with the issue of Kevin getting his taxes done, the first thing he had to do (after deciding to solve this problem), was to get help. So in the first week, his "homework" was to ask friends for referrals to get the names and contact info of three accountants.

That may sound like a very small step, but when something is overwhelming to you and you've been putting it off for years, the best way to pound it out is to whittle it down into baby steps.

For months, every week, Chelsea and Kevin would each have small actions to take and they made progress on the practical stuff until big things got done. But the real issues for them were much deeper than taxes or filing paperwork.

Lack of communication, blame, resentment, and not taking personal responsibility were the core issues at play here. The avoiding had to stop, and of course in order to transform their relationship, they had to face these issues.

I gave them a weekly exercise to do together that, according to them, saved their marriage. Back then I didn't have a name for it, but today I call it the "One **CHAT** Weekly Format." Each week for fifteen minutes only, they would talk to each other about money.

There were three rules they had to follow:

1. No Judging
2. No Blaming
3. No Excuses

With these three rules as the law of the land, they would each go through the formula:

C - Compliment
Give the other person a genuine compliment.
i.e. *Honey, you're doing a great job paying the bills each month.*

H - Higher standard
How can I hold myself to a higher standard?
i.e. *I will admit when I make mistakes, instead of defending my actions.*

A - Action

What action will I take this week?
i.e. *I will call the accountant on Thursday at 2pm.*

T - Truth
Reveal a truth to your partner.
i.e. *I'm scared that we may owe thousands of dollars to the government.*

These rules and this formula, and their commitment to having their weekly chats, gave them a safe place to face their issues without judgment, blame or excuses. And even though some weeks they didn't even talk much about money, this new pattern of communication with each other and with themselves completely shifted their financial situation and re-ignited their passion, solidifying their relationship.

Neither one of them changed or fixed the other person. As the judging, blaming and excuses dissipated, they each began to take full responsibility for their part in the situation. When you take responsibility for everything in your life, you have the power to design your life. And this is exactly what Chelsea and Kevin did.

If you don't have a partner, you can still do this exercise on your own. Why not give yourself a compliment, decide how you can hold yourself to a higher standard, commit to taking one action step, and be honest with yourself by admitting a mistake or recognizing a feeling that needs to be addressed.

How To Use This Strategy

Once you've recognized your issues by knowing your money type and recognizing patterns associated with that type (or types), use these strategies I just laid out for you to overcome them.

Let me give you one more example, so you can apply this immediately.

One obvious behavioral issue our friend, Spendthrift Sally, has is that she spends too much money. Now, I am not judging her and if this is you, do not judge yourself. (Remember, no judging). I have had many clients who both made and spent a quarter of a million or half a million dollars a year. And believe it or not, I didn't tell them to stop spending money. It's not my choice, it's theirs.

Spendthrift Sallys spend a lot of money on clothes, electronics, vacations, or "stuff." My job is not to judge them. In fact, *spending is only an issue* if it's an issue for them. If it makes them feel bad about themselves, causes fights with their partner, or if it prevents them from having what they want now or in the future, then it's an issue. (These deeper issues were all problems for Chelsea and Kevin.)

Most people have at least some of Spendthrift Sally in them. Our culture has contributed to creating mostly Spendthrift Sallys, Avoider Als and Delusional Dans. Haven't you heard these types of sentiments: "Buy it, you deserve it" or "Don't talk about money, it's a personal subject." Or that [insert expensive material item here] makes you look great!"

So most people, regardless of the money they have, overspend their money and have little to show for themselves at the end of the day.

In fact, most of my clients earn solid 6-figure incomes, but feel like they're stuck in the rat race and they don't know why. Often, they don't know how to turn it around. They think, *"I work hard, I earn good money, how come I feel like I still don't have enough?!"*

Spending of course is not inherently bad. Far from it, in fact—it's important and necessary. So don't judge yourself if you spend a lot, or have nothing to show for yourself at the end of the month. That will just stress you out more.

Instead, face your issues so you can make new choices, better choices, so you can get eliminate stress and get what you really want. So you can reach your goals, so you can live the life you deserve—not just today, but in the future as well.

Isolate The Issue

So ask yourself, *what's the real issue?* Do you spend too much? Do you make too little? Do you procrastinate? Do you feel guilty after spending? Do you get angry and blame yourself? Do you blame others? Do you buy when you don't have the money to fill a void? Is your marriage falling apart because you can't control your spending habits? Are you so deep in debt that you've given up?

Even if every single one of these problems are core issues, choose one to focus on. Isolate the issue.

Let's say the issue you will focus on is a behavioral one - you simply spend too much.

Decide To Solve it

Changing a pattern you've likely been running for decades isn't necessarily going to feel good, so you have to decide that this is an issue you will solve. You need to commit to changing your behavior.

You might simply say to yourself: *I am committed to spending less money this month.*

Take Action

What's the first step you will take? Well, how will you even know if you spend less this month or not, without knowing what you spent last month? You will need to have clarity about your spending, so at a minimum calculate what you spent last month. If this is too overwhelming, whittle it down and start with one baby step - print out your credit card statement. If this is too simple, fill out the Money MaSK™ worksheet.

Of course, if you've already done that, just take the next step, which could be anything to make sure you don't spend like you usually do. (i.e. don't bring money to the mall, keep a tally of your spending as you go, use coupons, etc.) Knowing what to do has not been the problem. You know how to spend less. Committing to doing so and taking action to support your commitment is all you need. (You'll learn more on taking appropriate action in Chapter 9.)

I used this strategy with a couple who appeared on an episode of The Financial G-Spot called, "Fifty Shades of Money."

As business partners in a romantic relationship, they had quite a few issues. Then near the end of the show, the woman turned to her boyfriend and said, "Should I tell her the truth" and continued to reveal that she was also in a relationship with a woman.

It's hard for anyone to try to solve a bunch of issues at once and these were some complicated issues. This strategy came in handy. They had to isolate the issues, decide to solve it and take action. Unfortunately, they got stuck on deciding to solve it and I'm not sure if they ever took action. Hopefully, I'll get them back on my show soon, so we can all find out the juicy end to this story.

Follow The Rules

As you face your issues and begin to take action, keep in mind those three rules I discussed earlier. No judging, no blaming, no excuses. This includes no judging or blaming yourself or others and no making excuses to yourself or to others. Following these rules alone, though extremely rudimentary, can completely transform your financial situation and your life.

As you face the truth about your money, take responsibility and let go of judgment, blame and excuses, you're giving yourself the keys to freedom, security, and an awesome life on your *terms*. This is what puts you on the path to money mastery.

Facing your issues really works.

If you're like most people, you may think (consciously or unconsciously) that facing your money issues will make you more worried or anxious. But actually, quite the opposite is true.

Not dealing with your money issues is what actually gives you anxiety.

If you're an Avoider Al and not in the habit of looking at your money, you may think looking at it will give you anxiety. This may be true at first, but once you get into the habit of looking at your money all the time, you won't experience anxiety or stress like you used to. When there are no surprises, you don't experience the fight-or-flight response. You know what to expect and the changes are less dramatic.

As you become aware and consciously notice what you're not happy with in regards to money, you naturally begin to make shifts in your behaviors so that you take fewer actions that aren't serving you and more that will serve you.

For example, if you notice that you're in the hole by $200/month, you may decide not to eat out one night, or you might reconsider buying that sweater you're eyeing when you're at the mall. Knowing that you just need to save or make $200 to break even tends to influence you to make small changes, moving you closer to your goal.

If you're Delusional Dan and you keep telling yourself that your new business will make a million dollars a year, but your Money MaSK™ shows that you've never made over $3,000 a month, you can begin to face the issue that you tend to have lofty goals but not lofty enough plans to reach them.

This is not to say your goals are delusional. The delusional part is that you have no plan to make that million bucks, but you hope it will somehow just happen. If you have HUGE goals, you must take intentional, massive amounts of action to make your seemingly impossible dreams a reality.

My biggest issue, as a Cheap Chip, was that I used to feel anxious when I spent money. I especially felt this way when I spent my money on things that I didn't really value, like going out to eat.

I remember meeting up with a group of high school friends about ten years ago in San Francisco. We went to a Mexican restaurant with a big group and my friends were ordering appetizers and individual meals and margaritas. Lots of margaritas. I didn't even drink, so throughout the whole meal, I was stressing about the bill. I knew that at the end of the meal, we'd end up splitting this bill, and I was starting to add up in my head the worse case scenario. Will it cost me 50 bucks? 100 bucks?

At the time, I was a singer–songwriter and I didn't make a lot of money. I was a good saver, so I wasn't broke. In fact, I may have even had a lot more money than my friends who worked "normal" jobs. I knew that even a $100 meal wouldn't put a dent in my piggy bank, but I couldn't enjoy myself, or my friends, because I was so worried about the bill. I was sitting in my seat overridden with anxiety. My palms were sweaty, my tummy felt nervous, I was barely listening to the conversation and hardly noticing the laughs. I know I was not laughing.

In the end, I think it cost all of about $45 per person. So, get this, I was totally stressing out (for hours!) for $45 bucks. I usually spent about 20 to 25 bucks at a meal. So actually, I tortured myself over a whopping 20 bucks!

Seriously, I had money issues.

Though I recognized this that night, it wasn't until later (much later) after I had run that worry pattern so much and stopped wanting to go out with friends that I knew **I** had to change.

Sitting at home one night being "appropriate" with my money, while my friends were all out having fun, finally brought me to my senses. First, I realized that an extra $20, $30 or even $50 paying for more than my share would not ruin my savings plan. Secondly, I remembered that I liked these people and that I liked being generous. If I could shift my focus to being more like Overgenerous Olivia, I could enjoy myself and feel good that I was helping others.

I isolated the issue (anxiety about spending money was keeping me from having fun with my friends), I decided to solve it (I made a commitment to stop getting anxious about spending, by focusing on being more generous) and I took one action step.

So here's what I did. The next time I went out with a big group, and knew I'd get stuck paying for things I didn't order, I embraced it. I ordered an appetizer and insisted on paying for the whole thing, even if it was for the table and we all shared it. It was a baby step, but for me it was a paradigm shift.

I developed new patterns when I went out with friends, being more generous and focusing on giving, instead of being fair and equal. I stopped calculating every dollar. I stopped feeling angry that I might have to pay more than my share. I even started offering to pay more sometimes, because I knew there was probably someone who might have felt worry and anxiety like I used to.

If you work at it, your current issues will go away. But don't expect to get rid of problems all together. Now that I have more money, new issues like whether to invest in a rental property or into our business arise. At times, anxiety about making spending or investing decisions, creep in. But I'm able to recognize it and stop the pattern, because I face it head on and follow the strategy I outlined in this chapter.

Any money decision could be an issue, but the goal is to be in control - specifically of your emotions and how you feel. Regardless of the issue, you get to choose to turn any negative emotions around. Just follow the strategy: isolate the issue, decide to solve it and take action.

So here's the game plan: Face your issues. This way, they won't follow you around like a sickness or plague anymore. Bring your "stuff" into view so you can deal with it. Otherwise, it could cost you much more than dollars. It could cost you your health. It could cost you your relationship. It could cost you your happiness.

Action Step:

1. Isolate the Issue:
What's your biggest issue with money? Start by picking one. Also add a sentence about how it's holding you back.

_____

_____

_____

2. Decide to Solve It:
Make the decision now to solve this issue. Draw a line in the sand. Write down three reasons why you will no longer stand to have this in your life.

_____

_____

_____

3. Take Action:
What is the one thing you will do today to address this issue?

_____

_____

If you're in a relationship, share <u>at least</u> one money issue with your partner. Allow yourself to be vulnerable. It will pay off.

JOIN ME LIVE ON MY RADIO OR TV SHOW

One of the things I like to do is have LIVE
guests on my radio and TV Show.

So if you're interested at all in speaking with me personally, make sure you click below to get the bonuses, and respond quickly when I offer you a chance to be on one of my shows.
Register Here:

http://robyncrane.com/bookbonuses

STEP 5 ~

ACKNOWLEDGE YOUR
LIMITING BELIEFS

Maybe you've heard this before. If you have studied anything about personal growth, then you probably already know the importance of acknowledging your limiting beliefs. This is not about making your beliefs wrong. Resist the temptation to judge yourself or your beliefs! It's typical for people to see things as either being good or bad, right or wrong. Your beliefs are not good, bad, right or wrong.

Today, I'm challenging you to see your limiting beliefs as exactly what they are—just beliefs.

Things you most likely picked up from your parents and experiences when you were two or three years old. Isn't it crazy that the quality of your life is contingent upon these beliefs that you inherited (or unconsciously chose) as a toddler?!

There's no need to dwell on that and please don't blame your folks for planting limiting beliefs in your head.

But it is time to acknowledge them, so once again you can choose to make changes.

Think of any one of your limiting beliefs.

Maybe something like:

"I need a man to take care of me." Or, "I'm not good with money." Or, "I don't deserve to be rich." Or, "Rich people are greedy."

If you haven't thought of one, read on. You will. Here are several examples of beliefs associated with the different money types.

If you are like Spendthrift Sally, you might believe that someone else is going to take care of you so you don't have to worry about money. You'll just spend, spend, spend and assume that it's all going to work out. Someone (somewhere) has you covered.

You might believe that you *deserve* it, since you work really, really hard. Maybe you make six figures and you think that you *need* a really nice dress. You believe you need it, you want it and you deserve it.

Remember Brenda, the stay-at-home mom who was spending $2,000 a month on clothes? She held many of these beliefs—she absolutely believed that a man would take care of her and this was reinforced by her husband's high six-figure income.

Brenda believed that having material things spoke somehow of her status in life, convincing others as well as herself that all was well. She also had an overwhelming fear of loss. If she didn't buy it now—this item she wasn't even aware that she wanted a half hour ago—would be gone, or the sale would be over and she would miss out.

But chief among these beliefs, Brenda believed that because her husband was a Vice President with a very high salary, she and her family deserved to have whatever they wanted.

Your Money Beliefs Are Not Logical

It may seem obvious to you now that you are reading this how little logic money beliefs (or any beliefs for that matter) have. To a Cheap Chip, these beliefs might sound outright ridiculous, but to a Spendthrift Sally, or Delusional Dan, it may make perfect sense!

But these beliefs are not right or wrong. It doesn't matter if you think they're rational or irrational. If you believe them to be true, your behaviors reflect that. The question you need to ask yourself is: *is this particular belief holding me back in some way?* As you acknowledge your limiting belief, you will begin to notice its consequences in your life and how they may in fact contradict everything that you want.

Common Spendthrift Sally Limiting Beliefs

For example, Brenda, our token Spendthrift Sally, believed that her family deserved to be able to buy whatever they wanted. But because she was overspending, they had little left to save. If these spending patterns continued, they'd run out of money two years after her husband retired. So the belief that *"we deserve to buy whatever we want"* was not serving her or her family at the highest level.

Also, Brenda felt guilt and remorse every single day. When discussing this behavior aloud in my office, Brenda couldn't help but burst into tears. She took on so much stress and anxiety from making purchasing decisions, especially because she didn't bring in any income to the household. And until uncovering their Money MaSK™ and net worth, she didn't realize how greatly her actions affected her family's future. But of course, she wasn't even aware of these thoughts until she started to say them out loud.

Common Limiting Beliefs of Cheap Chip

Cheap Chip, to give another example, may hold the limiting belief that he doesn't (and never will have) enough. He keeps saying to himself (likely unconsciously), *"I don't have enough, I'll probably never have enough, so I have to keep my money because one day it will be gone."* If you're like Cheap Chip, you're afraid you're going to lose your money, or run out of money, or somehow be unable to earn it again.

The crazy thing is, these money patterns can show up REGARDLESS OF HOW MUCH (OR HOW LITTLE) MONEY YOU HAVE.

Take Will Smith for example. Yeah, I mean the dude from *Men In Black, "Gettin' Jiggy Wit It," The Fresh Prince of Bel-Air, The Pursuit Of Happiness, Hancock, Hitch, I Am Legend*, etc. *THAT* Will Smith. I am not going to go as far as claiming that this gentleman is "exactly" like Cheap Chip, because I don't know him personally. But in an interview with Oprah, Will Smith said that he wakes up in the middle of night sometimes, covered in sweat, completely stressed out, his body shaking, because of a fear and a feeling that he's poor, or might lose all his money.

According to Forbes.com, Will Smith is #75 on 'The World's Most Powerful Celebrities" with annual earnings of $32 million dollars from 2013-2014! Some sources say the man has a net worth of over $200 Million dollars! Yet he admits to anxiety-triggered money dreams. Even if his net worth was just a quarter of that, could you believe *he* has anxiety about money? Sounds nuts, right?

I mean, it may seem pretty obvious to *you and me* that this is an *unrealistic* fear for Will Smith to have. Let's face it, even if he lost all of his money, he's still an amazing talent who's in high demand. I'm sure he could drum up a million or two (or 20!) in a jiffy. I'm assuming that he knows *logically* that this is a ridiculous fear. But the fact remains, limiting money beliefs still haunt him at times. Beliefs are not driven by logic.

There's hope for Will, though. As you can see, Will Smith faced his issues and acknowledged his limiting beliefs to Oprah and the world, which puts him in control of them instead of being controlled *by* them.

Your limiting money beliefs control you, until you acknowledge them.

I want you to acknowledge your limiting beliefs about money so you have the power to get rid of any and all of those that are not serving you. This way you can let them go, and move faster towards what you want.

Sound good? Sound good, Will Smith?

Letter to Will Smith (as an aside)

Dear Will Smith,

When you read this book, call me.

First, I'd like to thank you for your honesty—sharing your challenges. Second, I'd like to thank you for all your great movies. Third, I'd like to hear that you made your kids read this book, like you made them read Rich Dad, Poor Dad.

Fourth, I'd like to set up a BBQ with the Crane and Smith family. I think we'll have a blast!

Love and Kisses,

Robyn

Common Limiting Beliefs of Overgenerous Olivia

If you're like Overgenerous Olivia, you might believe that you are not good enough. (We all believe that at times, by the way.) You might believe that you don't deserve to have money. That other people deserve it but you don't.

Also, you might believe that by giving away everything you have, you're showing how selfless you are. You might believe that it shows you care about others and that you serve and help them. You might argue that it makes you feel good. And while you may not realize this, you may like being a victim or a martyr.

How else would you describe someone like Sarah Jane, more interested in helping others through a TV show than focusing on her own financial security? She frequently said to herself, *"others need help more than I do"* or *"I'll be fine, everything will work out"* or *"it's self gratifying to give to others."*

Sure, you may get love and attention by giving to others, but if you're doing it at the expense of yourself, there's no way you feel as good as you say you do. Being a giver is awesome, I'd never want you to change that about yourself. Just begin to focus on the truth: You deserve wealth, and money will just enhance who you already are—a giver.

So check this out: When you have a ton of money, I mean, a boatload of money, you have so SO **SO** much more to give.

Lang Hancock, who became one of the richest men in Australia in the 1950's, said it perfectly:

"The best way to help the poor is not to become one of them."

For example, Oprah can give more because she has more. She has done amazing things in the world. She's built schools in Africa. She's given away cars to her entire studio audience, and she's donated millions of dollars toward providing better education for students who have merit but no means.

She has done such incredible things all because she has so much to give.

If you are like Overgenerous Olivia and you believe that you have to contribute, then please do yourself a favor: give more to yourself first. Then you can give even more to others.

This means, if you don't have much money, don't offer to pay for others. Put your money aside, build an emergency and retirement fund for yourself first—before you start giving it away. Or, in order to be able to give as much as you want, whenever you want, dramatically increase your income. Since you care about others so much, make your success a prerequisite to helping them. That'll motivate you to succeed quickly! You don't necessarily have to wait until you are completely financially secure to be charitable again, but you do need to create new habits. Save a certain dollar amount a percentage of your income monthly.

Measure and track your progress towards your financial goals and think about giving to others only when you know it's not sabotaging your future. Then, make the conscious decision to contribute and keep track of how much you give to others.

I'm sure you've heard this before: "In the event of an emergency, please put on your oxygen mask before assisting others." If you don't have the money you want now, nor have enough saved up for the future - this is an **EMERGENCY**! "Put on" your Money MaSK™, and when I say "put on" I mean increase what you Make, decrease what you Spend, and Keep WAY MORE—before assisting others!

Common Limiting Beliefs of Delusional Dan

How about Delusional Dan?

Well, he believes that in order to have friends, and look good, and especially to get ahead in this world, he has to act like he's successful already. If you're like Delusional Dan, you might feel that you need to demonstrate (by having expensive things) that you have a ton of money.

You might believe that having showy things, like a nice car and a big house makes you look super cool, or at least super successful. You believe that people won't like you or accept you if you don't have those things. That people will judge you and think less of you, if you have less.

But, my dear Dan, *you don't need the fancy stuff to be significant.*

Mother Teresa was an incredibly significant woman. Gandhi was an incredibly significant man. I don't know how much money they had, but I do know they changed the world. People like that are significant for who they are, and what they give, not for how much stuff they've accumulated.

Delusional Dans also tend to believe in "get rich quick" opportunities. They may believe that there's a secret key to the golden kingdom. They may believe that they are going to be rich, but having that assumption sometimes holds them back. This is because they don't necessarily take the appropriate action to get rich since they strongly believe it will just happen to them.

Acknowledging these beliefs (whichever ring true to you) will give you the power to change your situation. Until recognizing that you have Delusional Dan tendencies, these feelings of insignificance, unimportance or inadequacy may be buried deep.

Once you have clarity that you do buy things to compensate for having those feelings, your logical brain steps in to defend you. Consciously, you know that you are in fact significant, important, and adequate—and that people like you for you, not for the stuff you have. Once you recognize this, you can start to train your unconscious mind by shifting your beliefs, and this will of course influence you the next time you make a buying decision. You may think something like, *"I'm awesome without this stuff. I don't need it —and in fact, not buying it will make me more successful financially."*

Just food for thought, Delusional Dan.

Common Limiting Beliefs of Avoider Al

Last, but not least, is good ol' Avoider Al.

If you're acting like a blind man even though you have the ability to see, and you refuse to even **want to** see the truth, then you believe that by avoiding "it"(whatever "it" is) makes it go away. Or at least you believe, on some level, that avoiding "it" prevents pain. You believe that looking at your money or dealing with the truth will *only make things worse.* You may believe that you can't handle your money issues. You may believe that you're not good at money, so you turn a blind eye.

But you're lying to yourself!

You *can* handle it. You *are* good at it. And as you know, it ain't going away. It will always creep up on you eventually. Why not just smell the roses?

Katie believed it would be more painful to look at her money than to avoid it (she knew avoiding was painful too—she just assumed it to be less so). But to her pleasant surprise, once she began to look at her money, it actually became less and less painful and more and more empowering and even exciting. She started to shift her beliefs. She started to quickly believe, *"I can do this. This will work. I control my financial future!"*

All of the examples above are just *some of* the limiting beliefs that you might have. Maybe the ones I listed are not exact reflections of your own, but you should have no problem identifying at least one of your limiting beliefs. I'm sure, if you're honest with yourself, you have hundreds just like I—and Will Smith—do.

So, here's what I want you to do:

Action Step:

First, I want you to capture as many limiting beliefs as you can. You can use any of the examples from above that resonate with you and come up with your own. Sometimes is helps to think about what your parents used to say or what you think they believe. Most people adopt similar or the exact opposite beliefs of their parents, so calling up their beliefs can help you identify yours.

List several of your limiting beliefs.

_____

_____

_____

_____

_____

_____

_____

_____

Once you have your list, star the one that's holding you back most or any one belief that stands out to you.

Now take out a brand new blank sheet of paper. I'm not talking a tiny piece of paper or a post-it note. I'm talking about a whole sheet of paper. Note: you will need this for a second exercise near the end of the book. So, be sure it is a normal sized piece of paper, so you get the full effect.

Now, on this piece of paper write down <u>one</u> limiting belief. I know you have a ton, but use the one you starred or pick another one. You can always do this exercise again and again if you want, so start with one.

I'm going to write down one of mine.

Mine is:

"It's hard to make money."

You heard it here, folks! That's quite a limiting belief. One that, unchecked, will continue to create untold havoc in my personal and professional life.

What could happen if you were to believe, like I still do, that "it's hard to make money"? Well then, you might give up. You might feel unworthy. You might make excuses. You might take simple things and make them difficult. And on and on.

So write down your limiting belief.

Don't analyze it, like I used to, just write it down. Put it on that single sheet of paper, and save it, because you will need it later—towards the end of the book. For now, just set it aside or fold it up and tuck it into this book.

Who would have thought that acknowledging your limiting beliefs had anything to do with financial planning and money management?

I'm sure you see by now how extremely important this is to your financial success. As I discussed early on in the book, your beliefs affect your behaviors, which affects your bank account. Don't move on until you get this and go through the exercise.

If you have a partner, I challenge you to share your new discovery in a "hmm, isn't that interesting" sort of way. Just acknowledge it. No judging. No blaming. No excuses.

LET'S GET BUSY!

Do you like what you've read so far?
Well, how about watching, listening and interacting!
There are some cool training videos, step-by-step
exercises and a community of interesting people
I'd like to introduce you to visit:

http://robyncrane.com/bookbonuses

PART III:

WHERE YOU WANT TO BE

STEP 6 ~

DETERMINING WHAT YOU WANT

I'm sure I'm not the first person to tell you that you need to know what you want in order to get it. Yet going into this in depth is an extremely important part of financial planning, which many people miss, so stay with me!

Before I met my husband at age 32, I was single for 10 years. Not 1, but 10 years. I hated dating, but I did it anyway. How else was I going to meet my man?!?

Even though I did *a lot* of online dating and I met some nice guys here and there, I didn't meet the right person. I usually only went on one date or two, maybe an occasional third date—but that was it.

Then I started thinking:

> "What's wrong with me?
> Am I ever going to meet someone?
> Is it ever going to happen?
> Is it ever going to work out?"

Eventually, I'd stop myself from sinking further down the never-ending spiral of self-doubt. No matter how disenchanted I got, I just <u>refused</u> to believe that I wouldn't meet the man of my dreams.

<u>Testing The "Law of Attraction"</u>

First, I knew that I needed to start *believing* that love would come to me. It was a "law of attraction" thing. I even wrote a very positive song about it (that was much different from most of my songs during my singer-songwriter days, which were notoriously known as *cynical* love songs). This new song was called, *"My Love,"* and went like this:

My love isn't far – doodootdoo-oo
'Cause I'm opening my heart – doodootdootdoodootdoo-oo
Give my love and I'll be free – doodootdoo-oo
So LOVE - will come to me.

(To hear the song, go to www.robyncrane.com/my-love)

Finally, I started to BELIEVE that I could, and would, find my match.

In addition to the song, I broke down and made a hokey vision board. I cut out bunches of pictures from magazines and printed out images from the internet *(no I didn't Photoshop my face into them—that came years later)* and put them on a big poster—and then stuck it on my wall. I even found out which wall was best for *Feng Shui* and I made myself look at my poster every single day.

One of the pictures I put up in the "relationship section" of my vision board was a picture of a couple walking down the beach, holding hands with their daughter. I loved it. To me, it represented what I ultimately wanted: a family. *Someday.*

Little did I know that what I had depicted in that image would come true—*faster* than I ever imagined. Within a year, I met the man who is now my husband. Yes, he is the man of my dreams. He's *better* than I ever imagined. He's even better looking than I expected and has a great body to boot!

I didn't guess that he'd have blue eyes or grey hair (not that I didn't want a blue-eyed, grey-haired *man-sicle*); nor did I guess that he'd have a repertoire of silly expressions.
You know what else he had? That I hadn't planned for? A daughter. SURPRISE!

Yes, it was a HUGE bonus…but I never EVER would have guessed that my cut-out-image of a couple walking hand-in-hand on the beach with their little girl was going to manifest itself so soon!

On one of our first dates, I met Trevor at Half Moon Bay, in California, to watch his sister compete in a triathlon. Cheering his sister on as she finished the swimming portion of her race, Trevor and I were walking hand in hand, on the beach, with his 2-year old daughter, Phoenix Rose.

Two years later when my husband and I got married, we had two weddings. The first was in a synagogue in California near where I grew up. The second was two days later, on the beach in Hawaii. (Yes, both were awesome!) The funny thing, is I didn't make a connection between my vision board and either of these two beach-walk moments until a whole year *after* we were married.

Trevor and I were in the living room where some of our Hawaii photos hang on the wall. Looking at the photo of all three of us (me, my husband and Phoenix) holding hands on the beach, Trevor said, *"Hey, that photo looks exactly like the one you used to have on your vision board when we first met."*

I couldn't believe it. I grabbed my computer to look for the photo evidence of my vision board and how it compared the Hawaii photo. The vision board photo looked exactly like a silhouette of the photo of us walking down the beach at our second wedding in Hawaii. We still have it hanging in our house. It took about year for it to actually manifest, but after a *decade* of being single, I had my family.

Talk about getting two for the price of one! It was the most amazing gift ever. I didn't even *know* that I wanted a daughter, but apparently I did. I can't imagine having it any other way.

I was very specific (in my pictures at least), and got exactly what I asked for.

So here's your opportunity to get very clear about what you want. Be VERY specific. Make a vision board if you'd like, or at least write it down. (And be *careful* what you wish for. You just might get it.)

And, as you do this, ask yourself: "What is that *thing* going to give me?"

Often people will think they want to get married, or they want to have a nice big house, or want a vacation home on the Cape, or travel around the world. That's all great and you should absolutely have it if you want it.

You deserve to have everything you want. Everything.

But think about what you want now, and in the future (1, 3, 5 and 10+ years) and what each of those *thing*s are really going to *give* you.

I didn't just want a man, I wanted a family. I wanted the love, the connection, the security and the certainty that I wouldn't be alone anymore.

The reason it's so important to identify what you *really* want on a deeper level (i.e. the feeling you're after) is because by knowing this deep desire, you have a greater chance of reaching it, either through setting another goal, or even without reaching the actual "thing" goal. Also, knowing this gives you insight into who you need to become to attract the stuff you want.

In my example, meeting my husband did give me feelings of love, connection, security and certainty, but actually I began feeling those emotions well before I met Trevor. Even my song says, "give my love and I'll be free." I had to give love *first*, and feel certainty *first* that I would be in a phenomenal relationship, and all of that helped me attract my love.

Using the Money Types to Help
Identify Your Deep Desires:

<u>Spendthrift Sally</u>

What does Spendthrift Sally (Or Sal) want? Well, she wants to buy things. But why? What is it she (or possibly you) really want?

Often times, what Spendthrift Sallys really want is to feel good. They buy stuff that they believe will give them immediate gratification. Sometimes shopping is also used as a strategy to distract themselves from other things they don't want to focus on. They might think, *"I'm bored..."* Or, *"I'm stressed out... I'm depressed... I know, I'll go shopping!"*

But the carefree feeling they're really after might be called freedom, or escape, or certainty. If you are a Spendthrift Sally, what is it that shopping and buying things GIVES you?

Ultimately, if you want "freedom" for example, spending, spending, and spending some more will NOT give you what you are ultimately looking for. Often times, it's quite the opposite: spending less can help get you in control of your money, which is what I call freedom! (As opposed to your money controlling you.)

Spending less impulsively will also allow you to make a conscious choice when you buy, so that you don't go home feeling guilt and remorse. That's FREEDOM! And when you start racking up the savings and begin building your wealth, that taste of freedom will get richer and richer (literally).

Here's the great part, Spendthrift Sally. You can begin to experience freedom well before you have all the money in the world to shop 'til you drop. As you start to feel empowered by the power of choice, and simply believe that being in control of your money is freeing, you can start feeling freedom immediately.

Cheap Chip

Cheap Chips may want a certain amount of money in the bank, and they may even be clear about what that magic number is that will supposedly be enough. But what are they really after? Most likely, they're after security. Peace of mind. Some proof that they will never run out of money. But Cheap Chip, you can start feeling more secure today.

My dad, a self diagnosed Cheap Chip (though he hates the word "cheap"), used to be extremely concerned that he would outlive his money. Even though he had more than enough to support him and my mom until they were 150, he had an irrational fear that the money would somehow run out.

Once he became clear on what he really wanted—to have enough money to live comfortably forever so that he *feels* financial secure—then we could figure out a plan. I helped set my dad up with income producing investments and used protective strategies on his portfolio as well. As we went through worse case scenarios he began to realize logically that there was likely no way he and my mom could spend all their money. He felt peace of mind and security knowing this, and this was because he had been clear about what he wanted. Yes, the plan itself was important as well, but determining what he wanted and the feeling he wanted came first.

Now, my dad lives abundantly. He still is price-conscious (as am I), but he doesn't have anxiety over it. He often jokes saying, *"what the heck, let's buy it. It's just a little less inheritance for the kids."* Though according to my money type names, he'd still be classified as a Cheap Chip, he now believes himself to more accurately be a "Frugal Frank" instead, and rightly so.

Overgenerous Olivia

Overgenerous Olivias want to give and help people. What is the deep desire they're after? They may do this to feel like they've made a difference in this world or possibly just to feel better about themselves (more important, more significant, more connected to others). Or sometimes they give in order to get others to like them.

Treating people, giving gifts and even lending (or simply giving) money to friends or family may make them feel loved and generous in the moment. But when they get depressed, upset or embarrassed when looking at their own finances, and when they lie to themselves by saying *"it'll just work out,"* they are actually far from reaching their potential to change the world.

As Ghandi so perfectly stated:

$$\text{"Be the change you wish}$$
$$\text{to see in the world."}$$

It takes getting clarity about your money and facing your issues to see that <u>not</u> taking care of yourself hinders your ultimate goal of helping people. As you change yourself, you will witness the value you give to others grow exponentially. This includes going deep within, finding the value you give others without giving them money, gifts, or even your time.

Overgenerous Olivia, you can make a much bigger difference in this world if you had money and more confidence in yourself. Focus on how much more you could help others if you were financially free and that will drive you to focus on yourself.

Delusional Dan

Delusional Dans want material things superficially, but often what they really want is status, significance or maybe even to feel beautiful inside (by looking beautiful on the outside). Typically, they also want to feel like they're important and/or unique.

Delusional Dan, you can be resourceful and feel important in ways other than having material things, especially when you know that those things are not appropriate for you to buy. The high you get from having stuff is fleeting. You can feel significant and important by borrowing some of Overgenerous Olivias' traits. Get involved in a charity. Volunteer to be on the board. You can immediately feel significant when you help others. Or, you can simply remind yourself that people like you for <u>you</u>, not for the stuff you have.

Avoider Al

Avoider Als generally want to enjoy life and feel good. They may want to feel calm, relaxed, and stress and worry-free.

Until reading this book, you may have pretended or convinced yourself that avoiding your money issues <u>does</u> make you feel good, or at least does make you feel better. By now, hopefully you're well aware of the underlying feelings of stress and fear that you keep buried down deep.

I already told you (using Katie as an example) how Avoider Als get the exact feeling they want by facing the things they're most fearful about. Completing the action steps in this book is exactly what you need to do to experience the feelings you want.

That also goes for each of the money types explained here. But only *you* can know what *you* really want—specifically the feelings you want to experience—and by identifying these feelings, you have the choice to start feeling that way today by employing different strategies.

In simple terms, find ways to experience your deepest desires from within. Make a conscious choice to feel the way you want to feel without spending, hoarding, giving or avoiding—and you will attract much more than wealth.

Wealth is not just about how much money you have. Wealth also means "abundant supply" (according to the Webster's dictionary). Truly wealthy people are wealthy because they feel abundant in many areas of their lives, not just in finance. You don't need to wait for the money to arrive in order to feel abundant. You can have an abundant supply of gratitude, love, happiness and fulfillment before your money changes at all.

> Determine what you want - especially the
> feeling you want to experience - and find
> a way to start experiencing it now.

Making it Happen

So go ahead and write down what you want. Include everything; your career goals, the amount of money you want, where you want to travel, what you'd like to give to your kids. Write it all down. Then take a moment to reflect on and capture the actual feeling you will have once you've gotten those things.

Maybe achieving your goal is going to give you freedom, security, peace of mind, love, significance, certainty, confidence, growth, self esteem, better health...or maybe something entirely different, like a sense of purpose. Whatever it is that you are going to get out of that thing you want, make sure to write that down too. *How is it going to make you feel?*

By the way, I also covered career goals on my vision board. I put down how much money I wanted to make, the millions of assets I would manage for my clients, the type clients I would have, the cool places I would speak, and who I'd share the stage with. But ultimately, what I wanted most was to *transform lives*. Once I realized this, I knew what I had to do. I knew coaching and speaking and writing would help me make the biggest impact. Today, I am so, so, so blessed that I get to do that every single day of my life! I had written down that I wanted to be a speaker and lead seminars, and I get to do that too. I wrote down all the specifics. For me, I knew it had to be an *ultimate* and *ideal* goal, *a mission*, because for me it was never about money, and it's never been about fame.

For me, it's about living my purpose.

So I had to think, "What is the *feeling* that I want?" I wanted (and still want) to make a difference—which you may relate to.

The fact is, that when I focus on helping people and making a difference, I make plenty of money anyway. I believe that the amount of money you make is in direct proportion to the number of people you help and the value you provide.

So, as I began to focus more on what I *really* wanted, which was to help more people and make a difference, I immediately began feeling more abundant, and amazingly enough, the money flowed in even faster.

Whatever your goals may be, make sure you're clear about what it is that you ultimately want.

Consider what the *stuff* or the *experiences* are going to give you. That way, if you don't get the *stuff*, you know what you're *really after* and you can go get it some other way. For instance, if you want a Tesla sports car, and upon further examination you realize you seek the feeling of helping the environment, you can take another action to get that same feeling, such as recycling or teaching others to save energy. Even before you have the money for that car, you can feel like you're making a difference in the environment. And at that point, you may not even want the car.

If you still want the Tesla, you can figure out the logistics of getting it: By when do you want the car, and how are you going to get an extra, say, $700 dollars a month? When you identify the end goal, you can work backwards to figure out how to get there.

Another way to start experiencing the deeper desire could be to do something for yourself spiritually, like meditation, yoga, writing, or even mindful thinking. It may sound airy-fairy to you, but we are powerful creatures. Your thoughts influence your feelings, and your feelings influence your beliefs, which influence your behaviors. All of this of course, affects your money.

If you are in a relationship, I suggest that you work on your vision together. It's great to understand what you really want first, but when it comes to creating a vision and putting it on paper, you and your honey should be aligned. A vision is much stronger and more compelling when two people want it and get to work together to get it.

One of my deepest desires is to have a phenomenal quality of life, which ultimately gives me the feeling of freedom and control to do what I want, when I want. Having this is reflected in the choices I make (and have made). Quality of life is not something you can outsource. I value it because it's about having enough time to do what means the most to me. My family and I have created and designed our quality of life. We travel a lot, we work when we want, and I get to make time for taking care of my health, like going to the chiropractor, acupuncturist or the gym.

I know I can work more and make even more money, but I always want to keep my ultimate desires of having a high quality of life and transforming lives at the forefront of my mind. I never want to lose sight of these desires or be working for the pure purpose of making more money.

Remain aware of your ultimate desires so that you don't sabotage your own fulfillment. Making and having money is great, but not at the detriment of creating the life you want.

So what do you want? In the next action step, you are going to write down all the things and stuff you want, and also capture the feeling or experience having that will give you.

Action Step:

Now it's time to capture *everything* you want and what having that will ultimately give you. Answer the questions below.

Here are some categories to help you brainstorm.

What do you want in the category of _____?

Money:

How much do you want to make? How much do you want to save? What do you want your net worth to be?

_____

_____

_____

_____

_____

Stuff:

What kind of stuff do you want? A helicopter, a 5-bedroom home?

_____

_____

_____

_____

_____

Quality Of Life

Next, think about quality of life: Do you want more time with your kids? To go on vacation? More flexibility in your job? Maybe a personal chef or someone to clean your home?

_____

_____

_____

_____

_____

2) Now, go back and read through each thing you write down make a list below of what having that will really give you. What are the emotions, feelings or experiences you'll get from having it?

Jot down anything that comes to mind. (i.e. "When I make $X/year, I'll feel _____," or "When I take a trip around the world, I'll experience these emotions…" or "When I have a personal chef, I'll experience _____" (Go ahead an make a long list, whatever flows out)

SOMETIMES IT JUST TAKES AN IDEA

The free guides walk you through lots of thought-provoking ideas that can help you come up with strategies to create fast results. Get the bonuses now:

http://robyncrane.com/bookbonuses

STEP 7 ~

ESTABLISH AND
MAINTAIN A SYSTEM

You were never taught a system for managing your money in school. If you're lucky, your parents had some sort of effective system for saving and spending, and you learned it by their example. But most people don't have an effective system.

What people do have are patterns.

Some patterns serve us.
Others do not.

You may not know it, but you have a specific pattern of doing things with your money, and I'm not just talking about your spending patterns. It's a "system" that controls how you think and what you do with your money. But, believe it or not, you also have a system that can set you free financially. You have a system that *you* can control. You have a system that you can use to help you manage your money more effectively and transform your life.

I only know this, because *I just gave it to you* in chapters two and three. Now you just have to use it.

This is what I call the KYM GYM™ system. It stands for Know Your Money to Grow Your Money.

The first part of the system is uncovering and tracking your Money MaSK™. How much you Make, Spend and Keep. Remember I said I would come back to this? By now, hopefully you've calculated it already, at least once. You've at least gotten a *general* idea of how much money comes in, where it's going, and how much is left (based on last month's numbers). It's probably not *exact* yet, and that's okay.

If you haven't done it yet, stop and do it now. Do not wait because then it will never happen.

You may have already noticed that uncovering your Money MaSK™ and calculating your net worth even once can instantly help you improve your financial situation. This is because your beliefs can change in an instant from a small shift in your behaviors, like looking at your money.

My guess is that just by reading this book, you've begun to *feel* different about money—and that is a huge transformation in itself!

However, *mastering* the system is not something that happens in one shot. To truly benefit from it, you must you monitor your progress from month to month. Three months of using this system consistently will begin to demonstrate the financial impact it can have. And using it forever can lead to a whole new life.

So your job is to keep this going. Have faith in the system and watch the magic reveal itself.

At a minimum, please commit to using the KYM GYM™ system for three months so you can see the incredible results of "knowing your money." Go ahead, try to prove me wrong—do it and tell me that knowing your money, which means having total clarity about the numbers, doesn't help you grow your money.

In fact, if you use this system for three months and don't see any financial benefit, I want you to contact me personally. Send me a message on Facebook and say to me, *"Robyn, I tracked my Money MaSK™ and net worth consistently and accurately for three months and got no result."* Then I will ask you to send me your numbers and I will give you a financial strategy session on me. I'm putting my time on the line here, my most valuable commodity, because I know this stuff works!

Remember, the more specific you are, the better your results will be. And the longer you track your money, the greater the transformation.

How Much You MAKE

Knowing what you make each month gives you the boundary for your spending (assuming you want to live within your means) until you make more money. There is no cap on your income. Even if you have a job, you can always find ways to make more money (getting a raise, having a side business, creating residual income streams). You may not *want* to do this—but don't lie to yourself and say you don't have a choice to increase what you make. (That would be a limiting belief.)

Use the downloadable Money MaSK™ worksheet (www.RobynCrane.com/templates) to capture your wages, bonuses, business income, interest income and miscellaneous income.

The income numbers to use here are "net" of taxes and other withholdings. An easy way to track this is to look at the amount of money that is deposited into your bank account from the first day of the month to the last day of the month. It's not your salary divided by twelve. It's what hits your bank account during the entire month. i.e. If you have a check that hasn't been cashed, don't count it. If you expect to get paid, but didn't yet, don't count that either.

How Much You SPEND

Getting a clear picture of the total amount you spend each month (and assuming you have clarity about how much you make) will show you immediately if you're spending less or more than you earn. That alone is valuable information to identify if overspending is one of your problems.

However, just knowing the <u>total</u> may not inspire you to change your habits. It's recognizing the specific choices you're making when it comes to spending that empowers you to make new choices. Thus, divide your expenses into categories so you can realize where your money is going and ask yourself if you really value what you are buying.

For example, Brenda (Spendthrift Sally) knew there was very little (if any) money left over at the end of the month. They were in the rat race, barely getting by with nothing left to save even though her husband made a great income. It wasn't until she tracked her Money MaSK™, specifically dividing their expenses into categories, that she and her husband realized where all the money was disappearing to. As you may remember one of the categories was clothing and the first month Brenda noticed that she was spending $2,000 in that category.

This revelation allowed Brenda to *choose* to continue the behavior or shift it. Upon realizing the actual amount she began to ask herself questions like, *"Do I value spending money on clothes? Do I need to spend this much each month to get what I want? Am I willing to cut back on these expenses so that we have more to save? What's an appropriate amount for me to spend on clothes?"*

One of the reasons that three months is a good amount of time to test this system is because it allows you to recognize trends. Like anything, if you have data from one time only (i.e. one month), you won't know if it's just an anomaly or if it's a common occurrence. (Even if it is a common occurrence you may unconsciously tell yourself something like, *"That was an unusual month,"* or *"I'm sure I don't always spend that much."* As you track your expenses month to month, you will recognize the actual trends and get a better picture of your spending tendencies.

Divide your expenses into categories that make sense to you. Keep it specific, but don't go overboard. For example, if you shop at

Target and sometimes buy groceries, clothes and household items, don't divide up one receipt into three categories. Just decide which category Target expenses will go under, like "household" (if that's typically the majority of your Target purchases) and be done with it. Keep it simple, but consistent. Whichever category you use for that store, stick to it so you can recognize ongoing trends and notice your progress.

Having total clarity about where every dollar you spend goes is extremely powerful. I can't emphasize enough how this simple discipline of categorization truly gives you more choices. By manually keeping track, you have a visceral experience, which is what drives you to change both your beliefs and behaviors. You may feel embarrassed that you spend so much money in one area. Or maybe you feel guilty. Or you might just feel totally empowered, seeing that you have a choice in regards to where you spend your money. This helps you consciously spend, instead of spending frivolously without intention.

Spend what you want. Just make sure you really want it.

How Much You KEEP (Savings Potential)

I also call this section your "savings potential," which includes what's left over at the end of the month and what you're currently saving towards your goals. Knowing what you keep is helpful because it gives you clarity on whether you have money to save, whether you have nothing left, or whether you're going deeper in the hole each month.

The amount left over at the end of the month, is called your "savings potential" because (assuming you do have money left) you'd now have the *potential to save* it to help you reach your goals. Growing this number, the amount you keep is what will allow you to make your money work for you.

At first, you may just keep it in your checking account as a buffer. But once you save consistently, month after month, you can choose to put a certain amount to work, so you can get what you want even faster. (Imagine being to able to have everything you want, that you wrote down in Step 6.)

For example, let's say in the first month you have $100 left. Second month, $200, and third month, $200 again. If you don't have an emergency or rainy day fund yet, you may start by automatically transferring $100 to your savings account to build it up. Three months of data is enough to show you the trend. In this case, you'd know that you can save $100 (at a minimum) consistently, so now you can commit to that.

If what you consistently keep is much higher, like $2,000 per month, you have the potential to save towards several of your goals. And now, you can use investment strategies to get that money working for you which are appropriate for your goals and time horizon.

Maybe you set up automatic payments of $500 into your emergency fund, $450 into your IRA and $800 into a brokerage account to go towards a down payment on a house. (The other $250 you may keep in your checking account as a buffer, in case you have less than $2,000 left in any given month.)

When you get these automatic payments set up, you begin to get in the habit of "paying yourself first." You won't have as much left in your checking account sitting there waiting for you to blow it. Instead, you will be getting closer and closer to reaching your goals.

The Money MaSK™ and Net Worth worksheets allow you to input data for one month. To get the full value of tracking your money, you must see the data side-by-side and evaluate your progress from month to month.

If you would like to use my entire KYM GYM™ system, which includes downloadable spreadsheets, video tutorials, a case study and workbook, then you may purchase it for only $29 here. www.RobynCrane.com/KYMGYM.

(Typically, this is only available as part of my *Money Mastery Home Study Course*, which retails for $1500.)

Train Your Brain

The goal of using this tracking system is to train your brain to make new choices that will move you *closer to* your financial goals, rather than *further from* them (which may be what's happening now).

Assuming you've decided that it's important to grow your money or even just have more money, your brain begins playing a game, and we all know that everyone likes to win. Isn't it true? Don't you want to win the money game? Wouldn't it be awesome to master your money so that it no longer controls you?

Well, this is exactly what using the KYM GYM™ system does for you. When you're tracking your money and evaluating it from month to month and you see that your savings potential is going up, you unconsciously (and likely consciously as well) want to continue to do that. As the number gets bigger you feel like you're winning, not losing—and so you will make changes in your behavior, like spending less or making more. You also have determined what you want and what having that will do for you (chapter 6), which acts as a magnet, pulling you closer to your goals. The combination of having clarity about your goals and clarity about your money trains your brain to take appropriate actions, which will help you reach your dreams.

Challenge yourself to track *every* dollar you make and *every* dollar you spend, consistently.

The easiest way to do this is to use a credit card or check card. Tracking cash does get very time consuming and tedious. Do your best to spend less than $200 in cash. Take notice of the exact amount you start with in your wallet at the beginning of the month (and how much you withdraw from the bank), so at a minimum you know how much cash you spend. If you can, keep the receipts and divide the expenses into categories. If that's just not plausible for you, put down the total cash amount in an "ATM" or "cash" category. If you're spending much more in cash than a couple hundred bucks, either stop and use a check card instead, or keep all your receipts. No matter how you slice it, every dollar should be accounted for, even if the category it's put into is not perfectly accurate.

Do the same with your net worth. Be accurate with your numbers by getting the values from your statements as of the last day of the month.

This discipline will virtually _transform_ your money situation.

Choose the date when you'd like to know your exact net worth each month. A great rule of thumb is to do this within the first ten days of each month. It gives you enough time to receive your statements in the mail or check them online.

The three-month rule applies here too. It takes about three months to be able to clearly identify a trend in your net worth. In three months, you can see which direction your money is going. Up or down (or staying the same). Many people begin to see changes after just one month, but the changes tend to be exponential. By six months, your Money MaSK™ or net worth may be virtually unrecognizable to you. You may be shocked by your numbers from months past.

Following this system will finally give you total clarity about your _real_ net worth. Not guessing and approximating, but KNOWING. You will find that KNOWING feels very good. And knowing your money is what motivates you to sacrifice some of the little things, so you can get the big payoff—financial security. Remember, no $5 Starbucks coffee or expensive dinner tastes as good as having more money feels!

The Benefits Of Using The KYM GYM System

Let me start with very simple numbers as an example:

Say you make $10. You spend $8. You keep $2.

Next month you make $10. You spend $7.50. You keep $2.50.

This is progress—you've now trained your brain to want to <u>keep</u> more money. So unconsciously you will do what you can the next month to keep even more.

Here is why tracking is so important:

If you notice you make $10 and consistently spend $11, then you are at negative 1, or losing $1. Through consciously and regularly noticing where your money goes, you are training your brain to keep a watchful eye on it so that you meet your goals. Even if you are only losing $1 a month, it may start to bother you. You might think, *"I don't want that to happen"* or *"No, it's going in the wrong direction!"* And it might motivate you to make shifts.

Evaluating these numbers is key. (This means look at the results, and *think* about what this means and how it affects your life.)

First, look at the bottom line: How much did you keep? Whether you have money left over, whether you are breaking even, or whether you're in the red (which means that you spent more than you made in a given month), knowing this number allows you to now *choose* what you'd like to change it to.

Below I used numbers that may make it easier for you to understand and see the impact. Disregard the fact that you make more, or make less than the example. It's just used to demonstrate the concepts and value of the system.

Example:

	JANUARY	FEBRUARY	MARCH
MAKE	$3,200.00	$3,200.00	$3,200.00
SPEND	$3,000.00	$3,200.00	$3,500.00
KEEP (Savings Potential)	($200.00)	($0.00)	(-$300.00)

Maybe you have $200 left over at the end of the month, but you'd like $1,000. Maybe if you had $1,000 you could save it towards a down payment on a new house, something very important to you and the quality of your life.

Maybe you're breaking even ($0) and you want to start saving into your emergency fund.

Or maybe you're going $300 in the hole every month.

Once you know where you are, you can decide what you want to save in order to make progress on getting where you want to be.

When you've chosen a savings (or "keep") goal, you can play the game of *lowering your expenses* or *increasing your income,* so you get to (and I love this part) KEEP more money!

With total clarity, you can begin to make changes in your beliefs and your behavior to help you get what you want.

Money MaSK™ Case Study

Here's an example of noticeable shifts that some past clients made in their first six months of working with me. Notice how the Money MaSK™ numbers give an indication of what changed from month to month. You can see how the numbers tell a story. Here, just from this summary, it's quite obvious what behaviors changed (mainly, the couple began spending less and then got a sizable tax return). If I were to show you the full spreadsheet in detail, you would quickly understand where specifically they cut spending.

	JANUARY	FEBRUARY	MARCH	APRIL	MAY	JUNE
MAKE	$10,244.00	$10,497.00	$10,452.00	$10,101.00	$24,077.00	$10,122.00
SPEND	$11,145.00	$9,721.00	$9,470.00	$10,604.00	$10,495.00	$9,266.00
KEEP (Savings Potential)	-$901.00	$776.00	$982.00	-$503.00	$13,582.00	$856.00

⇧	⇧	⇧	⇧	⇧	⇧
Started off spending more than they made	Became aware of overspending & spent less successfully	Continued spending less & began keeping more	Overspent this month	Received a sizable tax return	Continued saving at a consistent pace

This is what I mean by saying that when you pay attention to your money, you start to make shifts and things start to happen. This couple actually wasn't expecting a tax return at all, let alone a huge $13,000 "chunk of change." I'm not saying that tracking their money caused them to make an extra $13K, obviously their efforts since January had nothing to do with it. But, being aware of their money and their situation allowed them to make good use of the money, instead of just blowing it or letting it sit in their bank account doing nothing. That money ended up going towards a specific goal, invested in a strategic way to best help them reach their target more quickly.

Net Worth Case Study

Tracking your net worth and evaluating it monthly has a similar effect. To better understand the importance of knowing your net worth I used a balloon example. You don't want to *assume* that it goes down or goes up (like the balloon losing air, or gaining air), you need to look at the numbers and see <u>exactly</u> how much it goes up or down.

For example, if your net worth grows by a dollar and then next month grows by another dollar, then that is awesome. Or as our daughter would say, Gr-Awesome! (That's her made up word that combines Great and Awesome.)

You want it to keep growing!

As long as your money is going in the right direction (UP!) - you are making progress!

This means you're getting RICHER, instead of POORER.

If you aren't monitoring or watching your money and you don't see what's going on with your net worth, then your net worth could go down to 0 without you even noticing. Imagine you're balloon going *POP!*

Don't let that happen!

Got it? I really don't want your net worth to burst. I do not want it to suddenly pop, or shrivel down to nothing over time. I don't want you to lose track until you have nothing left by the time you are 65. The American Dream Education Campaign said that 40 percent of people in America have a net worth *less than, and* **never to exceed,** *$10,000!* Don't be part of that 40 percent.

Let me ask you a question. Do you think that wealthy people, let's say people who have over $1,000,000, have a system for keeping track of their money? I'll bet you a million bucks that they do! Because, that's HOW they stay wealthy. And that's how you can get wealthy. So how can you be more like wealthy people? One way is for you to establish and maintain a *proven* money system.

Remember Sophia, the young woman who increased her net worth by $30,000 in a day? Let's take a look at the rest of her story by looking at her net worth for three months.

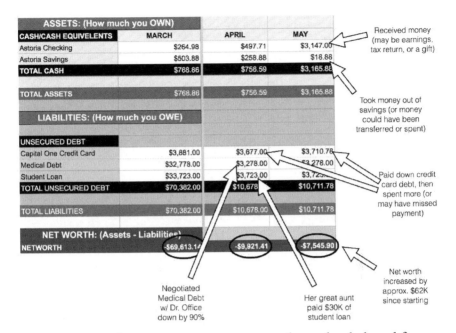

ASSETS: (How much you OWN)				
CASH/CASH EQUIVELENTS	MARCH	APRIL	MAY	Received money (may be earnings, tax return, or a gift)
Astoria Checking	$264.98	$497.71	$3,147.00	
Astoria Savings	$503.88	$258.88	$18.88	
TOTAL CASH	$768.86	$756.59	$3,165.88	
TOTAL ASSETS	$768.86	$756.59	$3,165.88	Took money out of savings (or money could have been transferred or spent)
LIABILITIES: (How much you OWE)				
UNSECURED DEBT				
Capital One Credit Card	$3,881.00	$3,677.00	$3,710.78	Paid down credit card debt, then spent more (or may have missed payment)
Medical Debt	$32,778.00	$3,278.00	$3,278.00	
Student Loan	$33,723.00	$3,723.00	$3,723.00	
TOTAL UNSECURED DEBT	$70,382.00	$10,678	$10,711.78	
TOTAL LIABILITIES	$70,382.00	$10,678.00	$10,711.78	
NET WORTH: (Assets - Liabilities)				
NETWORTH	-$69,613.14	-$9,921.41	-$7,545.90	Net worth increased by approx. $62K since starting

Negotiated Medical Debt w/ Dr. Office down by 90%

Her great aunt paid $30K of student loan

As you can see from my comments, so much can be deduced from looking at the numbers. The reason evaluating these numbers is so important is because you can directly see how your actions affect your money.

I told you that just by sharing her intention to get her finances in order, Sophia's great aunt offered to pay off her student loans. You may notice in the above chart that the full amount was not paid off. This is because Sophia wasn't totally clear about the loan balance when she had told her aunt, and so she guessed. It was close, but not knowing the exact number cost Sophia $3,723. Her aunt would have been happy to pay it, but of course, Sophia was so grateful for the incredibly generous gift, that she wasn't about to call up her aunt and say, "actually, can you give me another $3700, I was a little off."

As you can also see from the chart, Sophia increased her net worth by another $30K within the first month of us working together. She owed money to her doctor and before speaking to me, she had no idea that that debt could be negotiated. It took only a few phone calls to the doctor's billing department for them to knock off 90% of the debt just like that.

After just a few calls with me, and taking the new, unfamiliar and scary action of looking at her money, Sophia grew her net worth by about $60,000!

This is why I get paid the big bucks! ;)

Here's one more example of my private high-level clients, (let's call them Jen and Aaron) a couple in their early 40s who you may consider wealthy since their net worth was over $1 Million. Even though they had accumulated some wealth by an early age, they did not consider themselves financially secure.

They came to me for help for these main reasons:

1) They were spending more than they were making
2) They felt like they were in the rat race
3) They didn't have control of their money or emotions
4) They wanted to be a good example to their kids, so they could raise them to be financially responsible

They have a lot of different accounts, so I simplified it into categories.

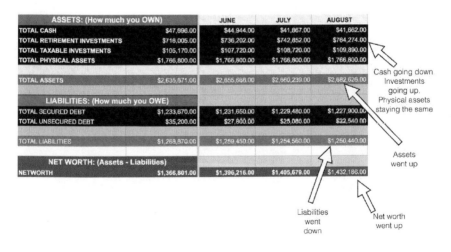

When looking at the net worth worksheet above, here are some simple things to notice.

In the assets category (what they OWN), the cash in their bank accounts was going down, their investments were going up and their physical assets (like their house and cars) stayed about the same. (technically, the value of their house was probably going up and the values of their cars were going down, but because it's so difficult to measure, we used the same value across the board to keep it simple)

In the liabilities category (what they OWE), they continued to decrease each month, which means they were paying down their debt instead of accumulating more.

Their net worth was going up.

Now, here's what's interesting.

I can get a very good picture of what happened, by looking at this. They used money in their bank accounts to pay down the debt and the market was going up. Had their investments not gone up, their net worth would have stayed about the same. And had their investments gone down, which it did do in the second half of the year, their net worth would have gone down (which it did).

Look, you may be in a similar situation as Sophia in the first example and not have a lot of money, or you may have a lot more like Jen and Aaron. What's amazing about this system is that it shows you what's happening with your money from month to month, so you can easily know where to focus.

I didn't give you the full picture of Jen and Aaron's situation and without all the numbers, you can't see all that's going on. I mentioned that one reason they came to me was because they were spending more than they were making.

Their Money MaSK™ showed me that they were spending $2-$5,000 more than they were making every single month. When looking at their expenses, they all seemed legitimate. Their fixed expenses alone were over $10,000. They had a mortgage, property tax, utilities, car payments, insurance premiums, school fees for their kids, etc. Even their variable expenses didn't seem so extravagant. They made over $300,000/year, it wasn't as if they were being totally irresponsible with their money. But everything adds up and every expense you have, or job you take, or investment strategy you use - is a choice. Each choice affects your money and affects your future.

You may have made some choices years ago, but *you* made the choice. And those choices affect you now, just as your current choices affect your future.

Jen and Aaron chose to buy a $1.7M dollar home in the Silicon Valley. They chose to finance a BMW and Honda CR-V. They chose to buy new clothes for their kids, and put their kids in daycare and make repairs or improvements on the house.
The KYM GYM™ system just shines a light on your choices and allows you to make new choices. Know your money to grow your money. This means get total clarity of the numbers, so you can make new choices that will help you grow your wealth.

Because they had a system, Jen and Aaron could see clearly how their choices were affecting their lives currently and how it would affect their lives in the future.

It took some time, but eventually they were able to:

1) Spend less than they made
2) Not just get by, but be able to save and get ahead
3) Get in control of their money and emotions, and
4) Be a great example to their kids as they pave a path to a solid financial secure

Track your Money MaSK™ and net worth.

That's all you need to start with in order to improve your financial situation. So write this one down. Put it on a sticky tab, make a giant poster of it. It doesn't matter, just remember this simple phrase:

Know Your Money to Grow Your Money
KYM GYM™

I know you have it here in the book, but I want you to see this everyday. To remember how important it is to KNOW YOUR MONEY!

Put it up on your mirror. Stick it on your refrigerator. Remind yourself to know your money.

When you know your money...*I am NOT making any promises here,* so I'll just say, when you know your money, *it tends* to grow. Not because of any "magic beans" out there, but because YOU can start to shift YOUR behaviors. You can start to shift your beliefs. Then your money can start to grow. Then you can have a magic beanstalk that reaches up into the sky towards your loftiest dreams, and your life can become incredible!

Take a moment to just imagine…

Imagine what it would be like if you *felt great* about your money. Imagine what it would be like if you felt like you *had more than enough* and you were more *in control* of your money and *not the least bit stressed out* about it. What else would be different for you? Do you think you might *behave* differently? Do you think you'd be more of a *pleasure to be around*?

What if you're in a relationship?

Assume you have now implemented a system and you have a proven process in place. Imagine how it might be to talk to your partner about money, as it grows and grows and grows. Imagine that it's not "his way" or "her way" or "my way." Imagine having a simple system that you implement *together*, and *look at regularly*. Imagine having a point of reference, a place to manage and measure what's happening with your money and a place to capture what you both want or don't want, now and in the future.

Imagine it being super simple.
Imagine it being empowering.

With those two things, the Money MaSK™ and net worth, you now have a system in place that you can start using, right... NOW! This is something you and your partner can look at together, talk about together, and use to build your vision together.

Congratulations, you are moving forward. I'm proud of you to have made it this far. Most people give up. Not you. You're here. You're going to make it. You deserve to have everything you want. You're awesome! (I just had to remind you of that!)

Action Step:

Schedule on your calendar times to spend filling in your Money MaSK™ and net worth.

Make sure you use numbers as of the last day of each month, and compare month to month to evaluate the changes. Then decide what changes you're willing to make. If you'd like the full KYM GYM™ system, which includes downloadable spreadsheets, video tutorials, a case study and workbook, then you may purchase it for only $29 here. www.RobynCrane.com/KYMGYM.

If you want to create your own, I'd recommend using an ongoing spreadsheet, so each month is laid out side by side. If you prefer paper, that's fine. Just keep it organized so it's easy to see changes from month to month and evaluate your progress.

BABY STEPS

We all have patterns that we run, and sometimes
it's hard to know where to start. That's one of
the reasons I created these bonuses for you.
If you haven't done so already, go here now:

http://robyncrane.com/bookbonuses

STEP 8 ~

SET TARGETS

Now that you know what you want and have a system in place, it's time to set targets. The great thing about a target is that it gives you something to shoot for.

Imagine we're going to play a game of darts. Assume that I give you the darts and tell you to go ahead and hit the target. Will you hit it? Not if I never brought out the dartboard! If you don't have a target, you can <u>guarantee</u> that you won't hit it, because there's nothing to hit!

Having a target gives you a nice bull's-eye at the very center at which to aim. But, better yet, it's okay if you don't hit it right in the center! In fact, most people throwing darts at a target miss the very center—most of the time. But, they keep throwing darts! You see, even getting *near* the bull's-eye is great, and the more you practice, the better you get at aiming and throwing, and the closer you get to the bull's-eye. Even when you don't hit it perfectly, you're making progress along the way.

There are many different types of targets, so to make it very easy for you, I've divided the "Money Targets" into three categories: "Money Ask", "Money MaSK™", and "Money Task" targets.

First you need to clarify what you want ("Money Ask" targets), next you must choose where you're going to get the money to pay for what you want—by making more or spending less ("Money MaSK™" targets) and finally, you have to specify what you need to do ("Money Task" targets) to hit the targets. Take a top-down approach when setting the targets and a bottom-up approach when taking action to hit them.

"Money Ask" Targets (Goals)

"Money Ask" targets, (also referred to as goals) are the targets you need to set in order to reach your 'thing' goals, or the stuff that you would <u>ask</u> for. Imagine you were still a little kid, and it's that special time of year when you get to "ask" Santa or Chanukah Harry or just your parents (if you grew up like I did) for the things you want. (Hopefully, you captured what you want in Chapter 6, but feel free to add more now).

Here are some examples of "ask" goals: Tesla, vacation home in Aspen, Jacuzzi, remodeled kitchen, vacation to Italy, personal chef, financial security in retirement, and so on. As you know, all of these things cost money.

The best way to increase your chances of hitting these targets is to identify the following:

1. **Identify the <u>specific</u> goal (what you want):**
   Don't just say a car, be specific. What year, make and model of car? i.e. 2015 Honda CR-V 2WD LX.

2. **Identify the cost (how much is it):** $23,445 (or $450/m for 60 months)
   To keep it simple, identify the cost either by the monthly amount that would come from your cash flow as an expense, or by the amount you need to save monthly in order to buy it by a certain time. For example, to finance or lease this car (with no down payment), it may cost $450/m. Or, you could buy the car outright, and you'd need to have $23,445 saved. So in order to get that amount, you need to figure out how much to save towards it each month in order to have enough by the time you want it. For example, if you want to buy it in 3 years, you need to save approximately $650/month (or $23,445 divided by 36 months).

3. **Identify the target purchase date (when do you want it by)** - Jan, 2, 2018

Action Step:

Pick your Top 5 "Money Ask" Targets and list them here (or on a separate sheet):

WHAT YOU WANT?	HOW MUCH IS IT?	WHEN DO YOU WANT IT?
i.e. Honda CR-V 2WD LX	$450/m	January, 2016
1)		
2)		
3)		
4)		
5)		

"Money MaSK™" Targets (Financial Targets)

According to the census bureau, in 2009, Americans spent $1.33 for every dollar that they earned. That means that Americans spent 33% more than they made that year.

So if you're like Spendthrift Sally or Delusional Dan, you are not alone.

Spending more than we earn has become part of our culture.

But it doesn't have to be this way. If you're unsatisfied with where you are financially, you need to set "Money MaSK™" targets, so that you have more money at the end of the month.

If you have a consistent salary, the easiest area to focus on is lowering expenses to increase your savings. But setting targets for each of the three areas may help you get creative to find ways to make more money too.

If you own your own business, it may make more sense to focus on increasing your revenue, but there's no doubt that lowering your expenses can also put more money in your pocket.

So go ahead and set financial targets for how much you want to <u>make</u>, <u>spend</u> and <u>keep</u> each month. Without a target, you don't know what to aim for and you don't know where to focus. If you don't have a target, you also don't know if you're making progress towards your goal (because you're not even clear what the specific goal is)!

Setting targets only works if you continue to pay attention to your money and measure your progress—so this is not a one-time deal. If you set targets and then you don't track your Money MaSK™, you won't clearly know how much progress you've made.

You must measure your results or you
will fall back into the same old patterns.

Action Step:

Start by setting targets in each area of the Money MaSK™.

First write down your current Money MaSK™ and next to it write down your new "Money MaSK™" target. To come up with your financial targets, start with how much you want to keep. Then decide if you're going to make more or spend less to get there and by how much.

	CURRENT MONEY MaSK	MONEY MaSK TARGET
MAKE	$_____	$_____
SPEND	$_____	$_____
KEEP	$_____	$_____

Example:

Let's assume a couple, Tim and Lisa take home $5,000 per month. (If you take home more or less than that, it doesn't matter. This is just a simple example to show you how this works). Assuming they spend $4800, they would keep $200 (or have $200 left to save towards their goals).

	CURRENT MONEY MaSK
MAKE	$5,000
SPEND	$4,800
KEEP	$200

They got these numbers by filling out their Money MaSK™ worksheet. See the detailed version on the next page.

How Much Do You MAKE?

NET INCOME	Use Monthly Numbers
Wages & Bonuses	$5,000.00
New side business	$0.00
Interest Income	$0.00
Investment Income	$0.00
Miscellaneous Income	$0.00
Spendable Income	$5,000.00

How Much Do You SPEND?

Fixed Expenses	
Rent or Monthly Mortgage Payment	$1,650.00
Gas & Electric	$100.00
Home phone/Internet	$50.00
Cell phone(s)	$200.00
Car payments	$300.00
Total Fixed Expenses	$2,300.00

Variable Expenses	
Entertainment & Eating Out	$800.00
Groceries	$400.00
Lunches and snacks/coffee	$150.00
Clothing	$150.00
Household items	$100.00
Auto Repairs/Maintenance/Fees	$50.00
Gasoline	$125.00
Out of pocket or after-tax medical	$90.00
Grooming (Hair, make-up)	$120.00
Pet food and grooming/boarding	$30.00
Fitness/Gym	$50.00
Landscaping/Gardening	$40.00
Student Loan Monthly Repayment	$250.00
Credit Card Monthly Minimum (if you carry a baland	$95.00
Vacations	$50.00
Total Variable Expenses	$2,500.00

Total Monthly Expenses	$4,800.00

How Much Do You Keep?

Your Savings Potential

$200.00

Let's say that after making their list of "Money Ask" targets above, they realize that to reach these goals, they need to be able to save $1,000, not $200. Now that they have clarity, they have a choice. Here are their options:

> 1) Change their "Money Ask" targets (i.e. change their goals to something less expensive, extend the time frame, or remove it altogether)
> 2) Increase how much they make, or
> 3) Decrease how much they spend

(A 4th option is always to do nothing and hope that it will just work out, but I want you to have the best chance of hitting your targets, so that option is out)!

Let's say Tim and Lisa decide to change their goals just slightly, and aim to have $900 leftover each month instead or $1000. The first choice they need to make is to decide to set a target for how much they make or how much they spend—or both—in order to come up with the extra $700/m, (since they keep $200 already). This will give them a total of $900.

Here's an example of Tim and Lisa's 'Current Money MaSK™' compared to their new "Money MaSK™" Target.

	CURRENT MONEY MaSK	MONEY MaSK TARGET
MAKE	$5,000	$5,300
SPEND	$4,800	$4,400
KEEP	$200	$900

Here, to hit their targets, they chose to focus on increasing their income by $300/m and decreasing their spending by $400/m.

If you haven't done it already, go back and fill in your 'Current Money MaSK™' and write down your make, spend and keep targets.

Once you've set these targets, the next step is to go deeper into your Money MaSK™ and set targets in the categories that you choose to focus on.

You may notice that you begin to ask yourself questions like, *"How can I make an extra $____ per month?"* or *"How can I save an extra $____ per month?"* These are quality questions and the more you ask, the more this record will play in your head and you'll start coming up with answers.

When it comes to spending, you might come up with the answer: *"I need to be on a budget,"* since that's something you've probably heard time and time again. But actually, I'm not telling you that you need a *budget*. I hate the word *budget*. Forget budgets. They don't work. People say, *"Oh, I need to get on a budget"* throughout their entire life—and it likely never ends up making them richer. I'm not going to tell you to get on a budget. Isn't that great news?

Budgets tend to take away the feeling that you have a choice.

It's almost as if you'd get in trouble if you veered from the budget. You might hear a motherly or fatherly voice inside your head say, *"You got off your budget again. Bad boy or Bad girl."*

Budgets have specific restrictions and rules—which in my mind, cuts out choice. You or someone else sets parameters, which you need to stay within. And if you do not stay within those parameters you might feel bad, or give up.

Targets inspire you to hit the bull's eye, but forgive you if you don't.

In fact, targets allow you to pay attention to your money without stifling your choices. However, if you set targets and continually miss them, you may be getting further and further away from your ultimate goals, such as getting out of debt or reaching financial freedom.

If you want to KEEP more money every month, which is really the only thing that will enable you to reach goals like paying off your debt or growing your money, then you need to either MAKE more or SPEND less. And you get to choose which of those you want to focus on and where specifically you want to focus.

Making shifts now, so you can have what you want *later*, is how you start building a solid financial future. Little shifts. Micro adjustments. Over time, they can have a MASSIVE impact.

Let's consider a couple of the Money Types again and how having financial targets can help them get what they ultimately want.

Spendthrift Sally, who would go on extravagant shopping sprees and then experience intense bouts of anxiety, really wanted a sense of freedom or to escape, and Cheap Chip, who lived in fear of spending money, ultimately wanted a sense of security. When they set "Money MaSK™" Targets—for example, Spendthrift Sally might set a target to spend $200 less on clothing per month, and Cheap Chip might take on a side job (or raise his current rates) to increase his monthly income by $500 and put more into retirement savings—they begin to access exactly what it is they were seeking (and never getting) through their unproductive and self-sabotaging behaviors.

Let me get specific again using the example of Tim and Lisa. Since they decided to increase their income by $300/m and decrease their spending by $400/m, they now need to look at their detailed Money MaSK™ that is divided into categories. With the data they have from tracking their Money MaSK™ for at least one month, they can now evaluate it and consider where they are willing to make changes.

In the spreadsheet below, the new column called, "Target" shows highlighted examples of how Tim and Lisa plan to make an extra $300/month and save an extra $400/month.

How Much Do You MAKE?

NET INCOME	Target	Use Monthly Numbers
Wages & Bonuses	$5,000.00	$5,000.00
New side business	$300.00	$0.00
Interest Income		$0.00
Investment Income		$0.00
Miscellaneous Income		$0.00
Spendable Income	$5,300.00	$5,000.00

How Much Do You SPEND?

Fixed Expenses	Target	
Rent or Monthly Mortgage Payment	$1,650.00	$1,650.00
Gas & Electric	$50.00	$100.00
Home phone/Internet	$50.00	$50.00
Cell phone(s)	$150.00	$200.00
Car payments	$300.00	$300.00
Total Fixed Expenses	$2,200.00	$2,300.00

Variable Expenses		
Entertainment & Eating Out	$700.00	$800.00
Groceries	$400.00	$400.00
Lunches and snacks/coffee	$50.00	$150.00
Clothing	$75.00	$150.00
Household items	$75.00	$100.00
Auto Repairs/Maintenance/Fees	$50.00	$50.00
Gasoline	$125.00	$125.00
Out of pocket or after-tax medical	$90.00	$90.00
Grooming (Hair, make-up)	$120.00	$120.00
Pet food and grooming/boarding	$30.00	$30.00
Fitness/Gym	$50.00	$50.00
Landscaping/Gardening	$40.00	$40.00
Student Loan Monthly Repayment	$250.00	$250.00
Credit Card Monthly Minimum (if you carry a balance	$95.00	$95.00
Vacations	$50.00	$50.00
Total Variable Expenses	$2,200.00	$2,500.00
Total Monthly Expenses	$4,400.00	$4,800.00

How Much Do You Keep?

Your Savings Potential

	Target	Use Monthly Numbers
	$900.00	$200.00

As you can see from above, in the income category, Tim and Lisa chose to make the extra $300/month from a new side business. To cut expenses by $400/month they decided to focus on changing their cell phone plan in order to save an extra $50/month and lowering their expenses in four of the variable categories which may not be as valuable to them as the others, or may just be easier to shift.

Now, you might look at this and say, *"Wait a minute, that looks like a budget."* But actually it's not. Here's why. The targets set here are intended to help Tim and Lisa reach their goal of saving $900/month instead of $200. By setting specific targets, they know what to focus on or pay attention to in order to hit the target. But the target of saving $900/month can be hit in many ways. If they don't hit their target of $700 in the "eating out" category, but lower their groceries by $100, they'll still hit their goal.

Also, they may not hit this target in the first month and that's okay. It might take them six months or even a year, which is why each month they continue to track their money, they can evaluate it and make changes, just as you need to do.

The important thing is to set your target and aim for it. What you will find is that merely being aware of your current spending will help you make new (and often better) choices.

This example might feel out of reach to you. Maybe you're going further into debt each month and the idea of saving $900/month is a total joke. If that's the case, your first target may just be to get even.

Maybe you're already saving a decent amount of money and feel like there's nothing left to save.

Regardless of your situation, there's always more to make and always more to save.

You just have to see everything as a choice. For example, you may choose to spend time with your family instead of working an extra 10 hours a week. You may choose to keep your car instead of selling it and taking the bus. You may choose to have a Smartphone. You may not want to change your choices, but the only way to be in control of your money is to have clarity about where it's going and see every choice you make—from what you earn to what you spend—as a choice.

I specifically gave this example of increasing savings to $900/m so that you can see how you might be able to save that amount or more, if you are compelled enough to do so. The reality is, most people need to save well over that amount in order to live as well in retirement as they do today. But the numbers are so overwhelming that most people don't even try. They just "do the best they can."

Let me give you an example, to give you an idea of how much you might need based on some assumptions. Let's assume you're 40 years old. So far, you've saved $50,000 and it's invested making 8% per year. Assume inflation is 3% per year. If your household makes $80,000/year and you want to have 80% of that income in retirement 25 years from now, you will need over $2.9 MILLION DOLLARS. (*Numbers from kiplinger.com retirement tool). I'm going to say that again.

$2.9 MILLION DOLLARS!!!

Want to guess how much you need to save each month over the next 25 years to get that massive amount of dough?

You'd need to save $2,169/month, and that will only last you 25 years— so don't plan on living longer than that!

If you're overwhelmed, freaked out, or just don't believe it, you're not alone. These retirement calculators have that effect on most people. But don't disregard it. This stuff is real. Check it out for yourself www.kiplinger.com, and select retirement tools.

It's important to mention that if you make more than $80K/year now and want to maintain a similar lifestyle in retirement, you'd need to save even more than $2,169 each month. and if you want an even better lifestyle, even more! If you make less, maybe you only need a million bucks.

Only a million?!?! Yes, I know it's crazy!

I'm bringing this up not to overwhelm you, but to empower you. And to give you a little kick in the butt. Using the KYM GYM™ system I shared with you (Step 7) coupled with setting your targets, will set you free. Don't expect to hit your targets overnight, but do expect to hit them.

You don't need to start working towards all your goals immediately. Start by setting "Money MaSK™" targets that are a little out of reach but truly achievable. Know what your ultimate target is (i.e. $2,169/month), but give yourself permission to move towards it, inch by inch. That's how it works, one step at a time.

Think of it as stair steps.

If you want to save $1,000/month, work up to it. Maybe you're going $100 in debt each month. So you might start with aiming to reach a savings potential of $300/month after 3 months, and $800 after 6 months. But in the first month, focus on breaking even.

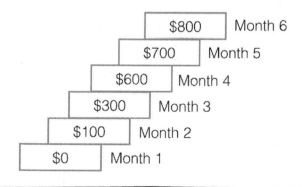

Remember, it's your choice. Now that you know what you want, you get to decide if you're willing to do what it takes to get there.

I'm assuming that you're here reading this book because ultimately, you want financial security, whatever that means to you. So if you want that, you have to work towards it, step by step, little by little, always keeping the vision of what you really want at the forefront of your mind.

When it comes to your money issues, progress is everything. Progress will make you feel better about the present and the future. Setting targets allows you to begin making progress—and before you even meet your targets, you'll begin to feel a sense of accomplishment from shifting your behaviors to work toward them.

Setting and moving toward your targets shows you that you have more control over your money than you thought. You also begin to get the wheels turning about what you'd like to have in the near and immediate future with that extra money. Begin asking yourself, "what would I like to have in the next 6 months, one year, ten years?" Building up an emergency fund to cover three months of expenses? Going on a nice family vacation? Paying for your children's college?

Here's the key:

As long as you set your targets, and measure your results, you will most likely improve.

Isn't that better than being on a budget? And setting financial targets is actually quite simple.

Now, you might be thinking, "Simple? Did she just say simple? That's not SIMPLE...that's HARD!"

If you're thinking that way, I understand. I used to make stuff like this hard also. But by setting small targets that I hit, or got close to, I was able to make progress that started to shift my money habits, which eventually changed my financial landscape.

Financial landscape! Sounds cool, right? Like a big field of money! Maybe even a mountain-scape of abundance!

If you make this into a game, you can have fun with it.

Life can be the same way. Play it like a game: <u>Set the target. Then, aim and shoot!</u>

This is your money game. Shoot for that target. Are you going to hit the target every time? No. Does that mean you should get mad at yourself and beat yourself up? No. You just try again. Pick up another dart and shoot.

You may rarely, if ever, hit the bull's-eye. Most of the time you'll miss, but the more you practice, the closer you'll get to hitting the bull's eye.

Whatever "Money MaSK™" targets you choose, make sure you don't set targets that you're not committed to hitting. It's okay to set mini targets and it's okay if you don't always hit them, but <u>create a plan</u> that includes specific action steps to help hit your targets, so at a minimum you move *closer* and *closer* to reaching your goals.

To give yourself a simple plan, ask yourself, *"What would have to happen for me to hit this target?"*

<u>Create A Winning Strategy</u>

You've set your targets, now you just need to create a winning strategy to hit them.

<u>Here are some examples:</u>

How can you spend less on eating out?

Maybe you decide you'll only eat out 3 times a week, instead of your normal 4 times a week. Or maybe you play a game of trying new restaurants that are less expensive. Or maybe you go to Group on and choose some new restaurants that have 50 percent off specials. Maybe you have some nice romantic dinners at home. Who knows? The <u>choice</u> is yours. You see, the main thing here is that you have CHOICES! Don't you love this?! Doesn't this now feel like you have MORE choices, rather than *less*?

If you're a Spendthrift Sally, focus on spending less money. One way to do that is to cut back on the compulsive and impulsive shopping.

I know you might have a weakness for shopping, but if you can cut down on your trips to the mall or your favorite stores, that will help you tremendously.

Or, if you value the shopping experience too much and minimizing shopping trips is not realistic, follow this fun exercise. I teach this technique to parents as something they can do with their kids who beg them to buy them stuff all the time. But it works for adults too. I call it a *"Shopping Discovery Trip."*

<u>Here's how it works:</u>

Go to the mall with your camera phone, but not your wallet (or be very disciplined and don't allow yourself to use it). Go to your favorite stores and take pictures of *everything* you'd like to buy: all the gorgeous shoes or dresses or electronics or gadgets. Make sure you take photos of the prices of each item as well.

Then go home and look through your pictures.

Ask yourself,

"What do I really want? What do I really need?

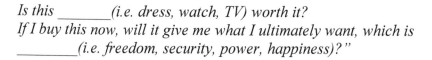

Is this _____(i.e. dress, watch, TV) worth it?
If I buy this now, will it give me what I ultimately want, which is
_____(i.e. freedom, security, power, happiness)?"

After all that if you want to go back to the mall to buy a few things, go ahead. But, I promise you, if you actually do this, you'll have a good chance of lowering your expenses and hitting your financial targets.

Cheap Chip might need to set different targets to create more abundance in his life. When I first became a financial planner, I was meeting with anyone for free. I'd sit with them for 2-3 hours, helping them with their money, hoping they'd eventually buy some product from me. I gave my time away for free, and because I didn't like to spend money, I assumed others didn't either. I assumed I wasn't worth the money.

It wasn't until I paid good money to hire a money coach that I was able to see that I too had value and in fact was valued more by my clients when they paid for my services. For Cheap Chip, you may want to focus on investing in yourself. You'll find that by investing in yourself, others will begin to invest in you and you'll make more money.

Overgenerous Olivia, you might focus on setting a target of keeping more of your money. You see, if you're tracking the amount of money you give away and spend on gifts, you'll be able to set a new target. Let's say you spent $500 last month on buying gifts for friends and treating people to lunch. Pick a new target for next month. If you lower that category to $300, you've just saved $200 bucks! Often being aware of your expenses in this area and setting a new target is enough to get you the result.

See how easy this is? It's all about focus and taking action, which I will expand on in the next chapter.

Delusional Dan, one of your targets may be lowering expenses in one area like Spendthrift Sally. Another may be increasing your income by let's say, $500. If you think big, you probably have a ton of ideas of how you can make more money. So pick one, and plan out how you will make that happen next month. I'm not saying this comes without sacrifice. But it is simple. If you have a 9 to 5 job and full weekend schedule with your kids, making an extra $500 might seem impossible, but it's not. You may need to wake up at 5am on the weekends, you may need to get on the computer after your kids go to bed. It may not be easy, but it is possible and something you can choose to do. People who live extraordinary lives do extraordinary things to make it happen. It won't just happen to you, but you can make it happen. Delusional Dans know this is true.

Avoider Al, you know what to do. Schedule time on your calendar to look at your money. If focusing on this for too long is just too painful, set a target of spending 15 minutes each week looking at your money. If it takes you a whole month to get your Money MaSK™ done, then take the whole month. Step outside your comfort zone little by little. You can make this happen. Please don't give up.

You can't give up. Please don't let this be another one of those times that you decided to get your finances in order and then didn't follow through. You got this.

Set your targets, create a simple plan to reach them, and then continue to measure your progress.

"Money Task" Targets (To Dos)

The purpose of setting "Money Task" targets is to identify what you need to do in order to hit your "Money MaSK™" targets, which of course enables you to hit your "Money Ask" targets.

I've given you many tasks to complete in this book. Whether you've completed them yet or not, many of them need to be done on an ongoing basis, so fill in the chart below and add other tasks that are relevant to you reaching your goals. (Other task examples: Filing your tax return, Saving into a retirement fund, Setting up a vacation fund, or you could even have a huge task like selling your home that you break up each step into small tasks).

Here's a simple formula I use with my clients to capture their list of tasks, the target deadline and the actual deadline. I simplify it as, 'what, what specifically, by when, by when really?'

WHAT?	WHAT SPECIFICALLY?	BY WHEN?	BY WHEN REALLY?

WHAT: What is it that you want to get done? i.e. Track my net worth

WHAT SPECIFICALLY: Write down the specific task you need to do <u>first.</u>

Maybe you have a bunch of different accounts and have no idea how to gather all your statements and it feels like it will take forever.

If a task seems overwhelming or you find that you're not doing it, break it down into smaller chunks. Decide what specifically to start with. For example, your first specific task may be just to gather your statements. These can be very simple, because as long as you set a new task target once this is complete, you will continue to make progress.

BY WHEN: Choose a deadline to complete the task. i.e. Thursday at 9pm

I know that for me, having a deadline is crucial. Otherwise, I'll always find something more important to do.

BY WHEN REALLY: Measure the actual completion date. i.e. Maybe you aimed to hit the target by Thursday at 9pm, but missed it. Instead of beating yourself up, just keep track of when you actually do get it done.

Here are examples of some "Money Task" targets just from the book. You fill out your deadlines and then write down the actual completion date.

WHAT?	WHAT SPECIFICALLY?	BY WHEN ?	BY WHEN REALLY?
Identify my Money Type.	Rate each Money Type on a scale of 1-10 and write down the top two		
Fill out Money MaSK worksheet	Print out bank and credit card statements from last month and fill in sheet.		
Calculate net worth	Gather statements (accounts, credit card statements, etc.)		
[Insert next "Money Task" target here.]			

Make sure you schedule your tasks on your calendar so they get done, especially for your most important ongoing tasks, like tracking your Money MaSK™ and net worth each month.

As always, if you're in a relationship, you get to work together on this. Choose some *specific* areas that you'd like to focus on with your partner. Set your targets and then measure your progress. You'll be amazed at how quickly you will get your finances in order and how easy it is to *get on the same page* and *play the money game* with your honey. Have fun!

Action Step:

Use the table below to continue your list of "Money Task" Targets. (Also, write this simple formula in a notebook or spreadsheet that you can continue to use on an ongoing basis).

WHAT?	WHAT SPECIFICALLY?	BY WHEN?	BY WHEN REALLY?

YOU'RE ALMOST THERE!

Sign up for the free book updates, training videos, access to my Radio and TV shows, and great free trainings!

http://robyncrane.com/bookbonuses

PART IV:

GETTING WHAT YOU WANT

STEP 9 ~

TAKE <u>APPROPRIATE</u> ACTION

You take action every minute of every day.

You're taking action right now by reading this book. You're taking action when you sit on the couch for hours watching TV or when you bust your butt to get a new job. The distinguishing factor here is the *type* of action you take and whether or not it will move you *closer to* what you ultimately want... *or further from it.*

When you take the *appropriate* action, it doesn't always feel good.

I want to make this very clear:

> Most people take actions that make them *feel* good in the moment; but they don't usually take actions that are really *good for them,* especially long term.

Getting Leverage

Brenda, for example, who shopped compulsively spending $2,000/month on clothes, felt good when she was on her shopping sprees. But later, that action backfired when she had feelings of guilt and remorse.

She didn't actually shift this behavior until she recognized the conflict: that the exact thing that made her feel good in the moment was preventing her from feeling good on a daily basis. The truth was, she was living in a world full of fear and anxiety, and she was ashamed that she and her family were barely getting by even though her husband made almost half a million dollars a year.

So what turned this all around?

The answer is simple: Leverage.

Leverage is the secret sauce you _need_ to take appropriate action and transform your life.

I first met Brenda when she attended one of my Money Parenting seminars, and Brenda decided; enough was _enough_. I was teaching parents how their beliefs and behaviors influence their kids' financial future. Brenda finally made the connection that it's not what she <u>says</u> to her children that will teach them how to feel about money or how to manage it. It is what she <u>does</u> that matters.

Her _actions_ influence her kids' actions, (just as your parents' actions influenced you and your actions influence your kids). Brenda's kids would model her behavior, as if given a specific formula. At the time, her formula was: overspend and feel good; then later get anxious and depressed. This was _not_ what she wanted to teach her kids! Once she felt the pain of passing down this behavior to her kids, she had enough leverage to ask for help. Without having first the awareness, and then the leverage to follow through and take new appropriate actions, she never would have changed.

You know what actions you need to take.

They are laid out here in this book, step by step. Unfortunately, up until now, something has been holding you back from taking <u>appropriate</u> actions to change your situation. _(And it's not just because you didn't know exactly what to do.)_

Why is that?

Well, it's because, up until now, you've associated more pain to doing these things than with not doing them. Avoiding pain is the strongest driving force for your actions. Secondarily, you will do things that give you pleasure.

Let's take Katie (Avoider Al) for example. Katie made the association or connection in her mind, that looking at her money was much more painful than not looking at her money so she just refused to do it. However, the result of avoiding her money gave her more of what she didn't want—missing credit card payments, going further into debt, feeling anxious and worthless. But, Katie disassociated from the pain by burying her head in the sand, because she refused to acknowledge the painful consequences of her ignorance. She lied to herself. *Sound familiar?*

Katie pretended everything would be okay. It wasn't until her money habits and emotions got so out of hand that she couldn't hide from them anymore. Already, at 27 years old, she was living with her mom and as her money situation worsened, and she imagined having to live there another 10 years —she finally had the leverage to change. For the first time in her life, the *reality* of her situation was more painful than the pain she *imagined* she would feel by facing the truth. That's when she asked for my help, and without the help, she probably would have slipped right back into her old Avoider Al patterns. Like most people, for Katie to truly transform, she not only needed leverage, she also needed accountability and coaching. With my help, she made a new association: Not looking at her money became associated with more pain than not looking at it. She was finally able to make progress.

Jim Rohn, a renowned author and motivational speaker said:

"We generally change ourselves for two reasons: inspiration or desperation."

You're probably reading this book either because you're inspired to change your situation or in desperate need of a change. Don't soften it by telling yourself, *"it just looked like a good read"* or, *"it doesn't hurt to learn more about money."*

Even if that *was* the case, and you picked up this book just to learn a bit more, if you truly want to change, which I know you must (or you wouldn't still be reading this), then you need to know the reasons *why* it is so important for you to change.

You have to convince yourself that not changing isn't an option anymore. You can't *kinda want to change* or think *it's a pretty good idea.* You need to be totally honest with yourself about what will happen if you don't take the appropriate action necessary to change.

Instead of waiting until things get really bad in your life, it's time to get real and honest about where your current actions are, or could be, taking you. Instead of telling yourself it will just work out, you have to imagine the worst possible consequences of your current actions. What would happen if you don't pay off your debt? If you'd had a tendency to be in debt your whole life, without drastic measures, you'll continue to be in debt the rest of your life. What would that be like? Will you get forced out of your home? Will you have to pay the credit card companies the first $1,000+ you make every month for the rest of your life? Will you have to work forever?

And what if you don't have enough saved for retirement? What will really happen? Will you be forced to live off a fixed income where you're in a crappy home you don't like, you can't afford to go out to eat, travel, or even be able to pay for your medications, or health needs? Will your kids need to take care of you?

If you allow yourself to go there and really experience the pain of what could happen, you then might have enough leverage to take appropriate action steps, even though it makes you uncomfortable.

But it's a MUST!

Stepping Outside Your Comfort Zone

Yes, it's time to get comfortable with being uncomfortable.

Robert Allen, author of *The One Minute Millionaire: The Enlightened Way to Wealth* said:

"Everything you want is outside your comfort zone."

I'll add to that. Everything you want, *that you don't already have,* is outside your comfort zone. Otherwise you'd already have it.

You say you don't want debt. But you're in debt because it's more comfortable for you to be in debt than it is for you to deal with your real money issues and make changes.

You might respond to that last statement saying, *"I'm not comfortable being in debt. I hate it."* Well, you must hate cutting back on your expenses even more. You hate putting yourself out there to do whatever it takes to make extra money even more. You hate feeling uncomfortable by starting a new business, asking for a raise, charging higher rates, asking a client for money, and so on — WAY MORE than being in debt. There are hundreds of conscious and unconscious reasons why you're staying in debt, so you need to see debt as even more painful and see financial freedom as even more compelling, in order to break the cycle.

I'm not saying all this to judge you or piss you off. I'm saying it to inspire you, to fire you up, to get you ready for change.

The "Lizard Brain"

I'm saying it because there's a part of your brain, often referred to as the "lizard brain" or "critter brain") whose job is to keep you safe. The lizard brain will do anything and everything to keep you safe, to keep you comfortable, even at the expense of sabotaging your success. It cares only about you surviving and couldn't care less about you thriving.

Once you've survived something, such as debt for example, your lizard brain is actually looking for it again. If you've successfully lived with debt, you're actually more comfortable being in debt than not being in debt. (This is unconscious, of course.) That part of your brain doesn't connect having what you haven't had (like wealth, or being debt-free) with safety. If you have never experienced having a lot of money or have had wealth, your lizard brain wants to keep you far from it! It's threatened by the idea. It thinks, *Debt = safety, so I need debt to be safe.* This sounds crazy, but it's true. It doesn't care about your success; it cares about your survival. You've only known getting by so debt and scarcity is the place of most comfort and familiarity to you. You don't associate survival or safety with wealth. And if you try to push past this limiting belief and change your behavior (i.e. by charging a new client more money, or asking for a raise) and you experience rejection, your lizard brain says, "see? that's proof that this is dangerous—time to flee and return to your old ways." Although its job is to protect you, your lizard brain is actually holding you back from having what you want.

Seth God in writes in his book, *Linchpin: Are you Indispensable?*

> "The lizard brain is the reason you're afraid, the
> reason you don't do all the art you can.... The
> lizard brain is the source of the resistance."

If the lizard brain doesn't fully equate financial security, or financial independence or financial abundance with safety, your lizard brain will keep you from having financial success.

So you must allow, even *force* yourself, to imagine the pain of what you *don't* want (i.e. debt or any other money challenge) to be so bad, so you get your brain to see that thing as UNSAFE. Similarly, you need to imagine the pleasure of what you *do* want (i.e. financial freedom, wealth, quality of life), to get your lizard brain to believe that it is something SAFE and survivable.

Initially, taking new actions, those that are best for you in the long run, will be uncomfortable.

Ultimately, when you commit to the appropriate actions that support you and your growth, you will get much more comfort, security and safety. The goal is to get this part of your brain on your side, and I'm going to show you how below. Once you do, you'll be in a position to get everything you want and deserve.

You deserve to have money. You deserve to have wealth. You deserve to have success. You deserve to have the quality of life that you love. Again, the way you will get all that is by taking new actions; new actions that may feel uncomfortable at first, at least in the moment.

Eventually, you will get the results you want by following through with each and every one of these new, appropriate action steps, no matter how hard and/or uncomfortable it gets.

Remember, how you support yourself in accomplishing this is by getting leverage.

The way you do that is by understanding WHY it is so important for you to change.

Making Associations That Motivate Change

Action Step:

First, make a list of the reasons why it is so important that you change.

Write on this page or take out a blank piece of paper and draw line down the middle of it from the top to the bottom. Now your page will be split into 2 columns. At the top of the left side of the page write: '*If I don't take appropriate action.*' At the top of the right side of the page, write : *How will this make me feel?*

On the left side, write down all the terrible things that *could* happen if you don't take appropriate action.

If I DON'T take appropriate action	How will this make me feel?
i.e. I'll go into MORE debt	angry
I'll be broke	helpless
It will ruin my relationship	devastated

Now, on a second sheet of paper (or in the book), make two columns again. On the left side write, *'When I do take appropriate action,'* and list what *could* happen, and again on the right, write down, 'How will this make me feel?'

When I DO take appropriate action:	How will this make me feel?
i.e. I'll have financial freedom	happy
I'll be in control of my money	empowered
It will enhance my relationship	fulfilled
_____	_____
_____	_____
_____	_____
_____	_____
_____	_____
_____	_____
_____	_____
_____	_____
_____	_____
_____	_____
_____	_____
_____	_____

With a long list of the pain you will experience if you don't change and the pleasure you will experience if you do change, you are intentionally cultivating feelings of both desperation and inspiration. When you imagine your situation spinning out of control, you are essentially being honest with yourself about the terrible things that could happen if you neglect to change. And when you imagine the wonderful rewards of financial freedom, you bring yourself to a place of total inspiration, which helps motivate you and compel you to take action.

Take a moment now to capture a few reasons why you must change, so you can look back at this when you don't *feel like* doing things like tracking your Money MaSK or calculating your net worth. Or, when you *feel like* doing things that aren't serving you like overspending or ignoring your money.

Write down here or on a separate piece of paper the top three reasons why you must change:

_____

_____

_____

_____

_____

_____

Annihilating Your Limiting Belief

Now that you've completed this exercise, you're ready to make a shift. You're about to take appropriate action to annihilate one of your limiting beliefs.

Remember that piece of paper from Chapter 5 with the limiting belief you wrote down? Well, it's time to take it out.

If you didn't do it yet, that's okay. Just take out a new piece of paper and on the sheet, write down one limiting belief. The one I used for myself was, *"It's hard to make money."*

You may be able to annihilate your belief just by doing this exercise once, or you may need to do it several times as you shift your behaviors as well and start to get new results. When most people have a challenge or an issue, they just wish it would go away…immediately, may be faster. Some people are all or nothing. When they set a target, they get impatient to try to hit it out of the park, right away and every time. I happen to be one of those people. I have a tendency to be a bit impatient. (Ask my husband.)

But please, pretty-please, try not to go from 0 to 100 so quickly. You've had patterns around money your entire life. Creating new patterns takes a little bit of time. I know, I want them to change overnight as well, but have patience.

It's all very simple, if you let it be simple. In fact, you'll actually have more sustainable results when you just take it one step at a time without expecting or judging anything. What's most important is that you acknowledge that this belief is no longer serving you. In this exercise you will find supporting evidence for why your belief actually doesn't make much sense or perhaps conflicts with other things you believe to be true, which will help you destroy the belief.

So, let's get this started by getting rid of that limiting belief that you wrote down on that full sheet of paper. Just entertain the idea that your belief may not be true, so you can begin to change the meaning and detach yourself from that belief. I know it might feel very real to you and completely justified. But the truth is, beliefs are just made-up. Have you ever believed something, really strongly, and later had a completely different belief? Of course you have. This happens to everyone of us all the time.

You may have at one time believed without a doubt in the Tooth Fairy, or Santa Claus, or if you were anything like my daughter, that you could fly.

You may have believed, as I used to, that you weren't smart or not good enough at something. But today, you know that that isn't (and wasn't ever) actually true.

People used to believe the world was flat. The idea of a round world was preposterous, until it was proven, and then like "that" people shifted their belief.

Before May 6, 1954 when Roger Bannister became the first person to run a 4-minute mile, people believed that it was impossible, that the human body was simply not capable of running a 4-minute mile.

However, the month after Roger achieved the "impossible", John Landy broke the barrier and within a few years, a dozen more runners did the same. Now, there are almost 900 men who have run a sub-4 minute mile, including a former high school student and a 40+ year-old man. (data from zenpsychiatry.com)

Whatever your belief about money, or your financial situation, or you and your capabilities, you must consider the likely possibility that these beliefs may not be true. That they're totally made up and you have power to completely shift any belief you choose.

For example, when I was a fanatical Cheap Chip, I fully believed that saving as much as possible meant that I would have more money. But that wasn't necessarily true. Once I began to bring more abundance into my life by letting go of anxiety and being less of a penny pincher, then I started making more money. Or course, saving less doesn't necessarily mean that you'll make more money, but in my case, being more abundant and generous with my money did result in me having more money. I started to see the value of living in abundance both emotionally and practically and it shifted my beliefs, which affected my behaviors. I went from believing *'I'd never have enough'* to believing *'I can always make more money,'* and then I did just that. I made more money, saved more money and grew my net worth.

So the point is:

Beliefs can be limiting. And sometimes, what you believe to be true—may not actually be true.

So let's start by getting rid of the one belief that you wrote down, that's no longer serving you.

Action Step:

First, write the limiting belief down here:

My old limiting belief is:

_____

_____

_____

Then, write down <u>three reasons why</u> that belief is totally bogus, completely false and utterly ridiculous. Basically, prove to yourself that that belief is a lie.

1. _____

2. _____

3. _____

Here's my example.

My old limiting belief is:

_____

"It's hard to make money."

Here's my rant giving three reasons WHY this belief is total B.S.

This is an outright lie that I *used* to tell myself. (Even if it was just a minute ago, it's in the past now!) There are so many reasons why this is just not a true statement, but I'll be very transparent here about why this is such B.S. for me specifically.

Number One: I make residual income

You see, one of the ways I earn money is through *residual* income. I am blessed to be a Certified Financial Planner™ practitioner. Over the years, I have developed and partnered with a money management team that helps protect and grow my clients' money, in any economy. How awesome is that?! Not only am I able to help people protect and grow their own money, I have also leveraged my time and the expertise of others to help me do it!

Here's what proves my belief to be a lie. I get paid a small fee for these services, four times a year. How can I say that is hard? It's not like I'm digging ditches for a living. Nor am I shoeing horses like my husband used to do when he was young. I'm very lucky. The truth is making money is not hard at all.

I get to do what I love to do every day. I get to serve and help people do things they don't necessarily like or understand, and I love to do it!

Number Two: I make money doing what I love.

I also get to earn money by coaching and speaking. To me it's the most fun, most rewarding, and one of the easiest things in the world for me to do. Why? Because it is my **passion**. I love coaching. I love transforming lives. I love to help someone, like you maybe, who may earn a lot of money but who still feels like they are struggling. Maybe you've been working 20 years or so, and maybe you think you have little to show for yourself. Maybe you're frustrated. Maybe you don't feel like you're in control of your money. So what do I do? I help you look at your Money MaSK™. I work with you (and possibly your partner) and we look at your net worth.

I work with you to help *face* and *get rid of* those issues that have been plaguing you for years.

Helping you turn your life (and your finances) around is what my life is all about. Be it through coaching or speaking, or this book, or any of my trainings, it's easy and fun for me. Best of all I get to serve and help people. In turn, they get so happy about the value they receive, they are grateful to pay for my assistance. Think about it: If you could invest $1, and get $3 to $5 or more in return, how often would you invest? How happy would you be?

So again, this <u>proves</u> that it is absolutely NOT hard to make money.

<u>Number Three: The easiest way I make money is when my husband makes money.</u>

I'm not on my own! Not only do I do *nothing* when he earns us money, but I get to *celebrate* when it goes into my (a-hem...*our*) bank account! All I have to do is look, and I can see that I've got some more money. It's the simple truth. Making money is not hard. My old limiting belief of *"It's hard to make money."* is utterly, and totally, and definitely untrue.

Now it's your turn.

I know it may seem ridiculous and you may not *feel like* doing this exercise, but force yourself to be uncomfortable. Instead of letting a new belief creep up like, *'this won't really help me at all,'* decide that this next exercise will help you. This is you proving to yourself that you can, will and must take new appropriate actions to transform your life.

Take that piece of paper, with your totally bogus, completely false, ridiculously imaginary limiting belief on it. As you say out loud your first reason why that belief is totally untrue, rip the page in half. Then as you rant about why it's total baloney, rip it in half again. Come on, rip that limiting belief to shreds, literally! Then say the next reason that the belief that's been plaguing you for years is just not true. Rip that piece of paper again and again as you prove to yourself that you will no longer stand for this false belief. Rip it up until that one piece of paper has been torn at least ten times and you've convinced yourself that that old belief is an outright lie.

As you rip up this old limiting belief, you're also telling your unconscious mind that you will <u>no longer stand for letting this stuff hold you back</u>! You are making a statement, drawing a line in the sand, saying, *"I will not be controlled by this old, disempowering, limiting belief any longer!"* This is a process of *acknowledging* that it has been holding you back, and *celebrating* that you are letting go of it.

Because it "is" total B.S.!

You've got to <u>prove</u> to your hardheaded mind that it is B.S. Prove to your brain, which usually finds evidence to support why your limiting belief is true, that it is wrong!

Don't let the part of your brain that wants to keep you safe control you.

All done? Awesome!

Action Step:

Now, write down your new belief, which you now know to be true.

My new belief is:

_____

_____

_____

_____

_____

_____

Here is my new empowering belief:

"It's easy to make money!"

Keep your itty-bitty pieces of torn-up paper handy (your old crappy limiting belief that used to hold you back) because you're going to need it in Step 10.

....

FINSH & FOLLOW-THROUGH

Most people don't finish what they start.
One of the primary reasons is because they
don't get the help they *really* need.
I'm here to help you:

http://robyncrane.com/bookbonuses

....

STEP 10 ~

SET YOURSELF UP FOR SUCCESS

You have been amazing. You made the decision and commitment to improve your money habits and here you are—on Step 10, following through. Step 10 is all about setting yourself up for success, so you can get fast and sustainable results. After reading this far, you now know <u>what</u> to do and <u>how</u> to do it, so you can make money work for you, get out of debt, relieve money stress and make financial planning easy.

This chapter will guide you on your path to money mastery and help you have long lasting success.

7 Tips to Long Lasting Success

1. Celebrate
2. Anticipate Challenges
3. Create Empowering Habits & Rituals
4. Get Leverage
5. Maintain a Wealthy Mindset
6. Work with a Money Coach
7. Take One Step at a Time

1. Celebrate

Celebrating is an essential part of success. If you don't take the time to celebrate and truly, wholeheartedly appreciate every little step of the way, you can easily sabotage your success. Everyone likes to be appreciated, but for some reason, we tend to forget how important it is to appreciate ourselves.

It sounds simple enough, to simply appreciate yourself and celebrate your small successes, but for some reason it's not always easy. If you're anything like *I used to be*, you don't take nearly enough time to celebrate. I hate to admit it, but that was one of my old patterns—beating myself up and making a case for why no matter what I did, wasn't enough. Or worse, focusing on everything I did *wrong* instead of all the things I did right.

You might run a similar pattern and focus on where you're falling short or put attention on what you haven't done—but believe me, this only holds you back from taking appropriate action and getting what you want. (By the way, even though I still run this pattern at times, I'm intentionally using the past tense so I continue to train my brain to celebrate as much as possible).

For example, maybe you haven't done all the exercises in this book yet, so you tell yourself you don't deserve to celebrate. Please, please don't do that. Don't come up with reasons why you don't deserve to celebrate.

Check it out: Even if this is the first sentence you've read in this whole book (thought that would be a little weird and unlikely) you would still deserve to celebrate, because you are taking action.

Unfortunately, when you don't take time to celebrate the *little things*, and all you do is stress out and worry, *which I used to do,* you miss the most important and most magical part of your life. The awesome, fantastic, miracle of: Right Now.

I'm talking:
This <u>very</u> minute.

Celebrating and being grateful for the now is something we all need more of. Maybe just picking this book up was a huge step for you and now here you are, reading it until the end. Maybe you became aware of your expenses and somehow spent a bit less money last month. Maybe you focused on making more money and you closed a new sale or are about to. Or maybe you've shifted the way you look at money or the way you feel about money. Maybe you feel more empowered and have faith that you control your

---

financial future. Any small shift in either your beliefs or behaviors can change the trajectory of your life. Where ever you are now, be grateful and celebrate it.

Continue to acknowledge yourself for every positive action you take toward your goal, and really mean it. Overcoming your money issues is a journey, so even if you're not ultimately where you want to be, I know that you've definitely made progress. And progress equals success!

Action Step:

What's one little thing you've shifted that you can appreciate yourself for right now?

Write it down here:

_____

_____

_____

Give yourself some love. You are awesome! Whoohoo!

(Yeah, I just said "Whoohoo." I'm excited for you, okay?)

The reason celebrating is paramount to your success in overcoming your money issues and having money mastery is because how you feel will determine what you do. You want to feel good and proud of the progress you're making, because that will motivate and inspire you to continue.

You see, there is a little kid in all of us. A little kid who needs to be nurtured, and supported, celebrated and loved. You wouldn't tell a little kid HALF of the awful stuff that you say to yourself on a regular basis. Things like, *"you're not good at money,"* or *"you don't deserve to be rich,"* or something like the one I used to nastily say to myself all the time, *"you're so stupid."*

You may not even notice that you say things like this to yourself. But you do.

The little kid inside of you needs to be rewarded for baby steps. Have you ever seen (or been) a parent with a little baby learning to walk? For each tiny, itsy-bitsy little movement forward, you cheer and celebrate and applaud. For some sad reason, we stop doing this, and don't take the time to celebrate ourselves.

You can celebrate by making a list of all the ways in which you're awesome. You can celebrate by bragging to your friend or your mom (I do both!). Or you can celebrate by jumping up and down like a cheerleader. Do it however you want, but take my word for it on this one, the more you change your physical state, the more of an impact it has on your unconscious mind. If you're hunched over mumbling to yourself in a soft tone, "I'm awesome," you're unconscious mind doesn't believe it. So the more the express your gratitude and appreciation for yourself physically (i.e standing tall, smiling, saying something with heart and pride), the more rewarded your mind feels and the more it will do to get the feeling again.

So let's give this "celebration thing" a whirl right now. Even if this is a bit uncomfortable—it's good practice, as you know. Stand up, take a deep breath, put your hands up in the air, and with some energy, say something like, "I am awesome!" or "I control my life!" or "I make great choices with my money," or "I have more abundance in my life everyday!"

Now grab that pile of little pieces of paper that you ripped up and follow along, you're going to use it as confetti. Hold it in your hand now and think of something you can celebrate and say it out loud as you throw a few of pieces up in the air. *(i.e. "I set my Money MaSK goals")* Say another thing you could celebrate and throw it up in the air, (i.e. *"I grew my net worth!"*) Now smile, act silly, or say something crazy like, "Woohoo!" and toss the rest of the confetti in the air. If you want to celebrate differently, go for it. I'd just encourage you to change your state and feel some excitement in your body. This will train your brain to take more appropriate action and get even faster results.

Enjoy yourself. Act like a little kid. Appreciate your efforts. Celebrate.

Look, I know there's something you really want, that you may think you need to get before you can celebrate. Maybe it's getting out of debt, maybe it's making 6 figures, or having a million dollars, or maybe it's reaching total financial freedom.

This is your life. You only get one. Please don't wait until you reach your goal to celebrate. You feel great about money well before you have all the money you want. You can feel free before you have financial freedom. You can feel secure before you have financial security. You can have peace of mind before you have total wealth.

Keep going after what you want and my challenge to you is to enjoy it—

Every step of the way.

2. Anticipate Your Challenges

Make no mistake: There will be challenges as you make real changes. It's also going to be uncomfortable because it's necessary to step outside your comfort zone to make new and different choices.

Henry Ford said,

"If you always do what you've always done, you'll always get what you've always got."

That concept is really applicable here. It's important to anticipate challenges you might face as you make changes. Remember, you've had a relationship with money almost your whole life. Your beliefs and behaviors were influenced by your parents, friends, environment and experiences. You have to expect that if you only change your money patterns, but not your surroundings, of course there are going to be some bumps along the road. Anticipate the challenges you may face so you can get ahead of them and have a plan in place for who and what will support your success when you're tempted to fall back into old patterns.

What challenges can you anticipate experiencing as you work to change your money habits? In a minute, I'm going to have you write some ideas down. For now, here are some common challenges I've seen that may apply to you: (to help jog your mind)

- You may get anxious, overwhelmed or nervous when looking at your money.
- You may feel you're too busy and don't have the time to manage your money or deal with this "right now."
- You might tell yourself you don't know how to track your money, feel that money confuses you or you might make excuses why you can't get it done (more on why a coach can be the remedy to this below).
- You might have people in your life who don't support your goals to have money mastery. They might say you don't need to worry about your money, that it will all work out, that you'll be fine.
- Your partner may not be on board or may be overspending, or money may be a tense subject between you, so you may ignore it to keep the peace.
- You might soften the reality of your situation and convince yourself you don't need to change.
- You might tell yourself all of your money issues will just resolve when you make more money *someday.*

- You might want to postpone working on your money issues until after the holidays, after your family vacation, after your next big deadline at work, after your health improves, after INSERT-THING.
- You just may not feel like focusing on your money — there's always something more urgent.
- At times, it may not feel good (i.e. you may have to make sacrifices or feel bad in the moment).

Some of these may be legitimate and true, but regardless, they're not going to get you the results you want. And they're not good enough reasons to avoid taking the actions that will change your life. You don't want to be in the exact same place you are now one year (or even 1 month) from today.

Action Step:

Put a star next to the potential challenges listed above that apply to you.

Write down 5 other challenges you expect to have when you begin to (or continue) to make shifts in your life.

1._____

2._____

3._____

4._____

5._____

Great job! (You're going to get a lot of celebration from me in this chapter.)

3. Create Empowering Habits and Rituals

Throughout the book as I used client examples of the different money types, you may have noticed how changes in their beliefs and behaviors were the impetus to jumpstart their financial success. Obviously, if their new beliefs and behaviors were short-lived, they would not have been able to maintain their success and in fact, most likely would have sabotaged it.

It was consistent implementation of these steps that allowed them to create new empowering habits and rituals. Having habits and rituals in place is what you need as well, not to only lock in the progress you've made, but also to create exponential results. Success builds on success and that has a compounding effect on your financial future.

Let's take a look at what some of my clients did and how they created new habits and rituals to help them succeed.

Our friend, Brenda (Spendthrift Sally) got very clear on her Money MaSK™. For the first time, she had total transparency when it came to her finances. She was clear about how much money was actually coming in each month and she noticed how much she was spending in each category, so she made new choices.

Brenda began consciously spending her money. She didn't stop spending money on the things that she valued, but she did spend much less on the things that she didn't value as much. For example, going on a very nice vacation each year was extremely important to her and her family. So they spent a generous amount of money on their vacations intentionally, and cut back on the clothes and kids' expenses that weren't as important. As she made these shifts, Brenda began to feel in control of her money. She didn't get stressed and anxious like she used to. She and her husband began working as a team and got on the same page about the future. Brenda didn't lose her love for shopping, but she did change her spending habits to be more like a *"Spend-wisely Sally."*

As a Cheap Chip, I still am conscious about what I spend, but I spend much more freely and with little worry. I began a new ritual of telling myself daily that it's easy to make money, and so it got easier. I found creative ways to make money, like turning our basement into an apartment and renting it out. So, at times, when I spend hundreds of dollars on eating out, (something that in the past would have given me a stroke) I feel no stress at all. I remember on one of my brother's birthdays, I said to myself as we paid the large bill, *"no biggie, that was covered from just a couple of days rent."* Now, I feel abundance in my life every day, and even though I still watch what I spend, just like my dad, I'm more of a *"**Frugal Frank**"* than a *Cheap Chip*.

Sarah Jane, who ranked highest as Overgenerous Olivia with Delusional Dan and Avoider Al as close runner ups, first had to face her money issues. She recognized that helping others had been a higher priority than helping herself and that her core beliefs about money were holding her back. Though we only reconnected one time shortly after *The Financial G-Spot* episode, she reported that she now has a note on her mirror that reads, *'The more money I have, the more I can give,'* to help her focus on making more money and saving more for her own retirement. Sarah Jane also now has more clarity about her income and saving goals and is working hard to increase her earnings. With a simple ritual of reading those words on her mirror and a more challenging habit of tracking her Money MaSK™, Sarah Jane is on the road to a more successful financial future. She's turning into a *"**Conscientious Connie.**"*

Matt, (Delusional Dan) the police officer who owned his own business, had BIG dreams and began taking serious action. After working with me, he hired a phenomenal business consultant (my husband, Trevor) and launched a new development company. Within his first eighteen months in the new business, Matt's company owned over $20 million in assets. This is the kind of thing Delusional Dan is capable of when he creates habits of taking action and following through. Let's give him a new name too: ***"Action-Taker Andy."***

Katie, our Avoider Al who represents a part of all of us, is a changed person. She now believes without a shadow of a doubt that facing her money issues and looking at her money are essential to her financial success. She also believes that this is what dictates the quality of her life.

Katie is now very conscious about the choices she makes when spending her money. A new habit she adopted is to consider value when spending her money and though she's not perfect about it, she's much better at looking at her money and tracking her Money MaSK™. She recently received $4,000 of additional income. In the past, she would have just blown this money in a heartbeat. The Avoider Al in her would have felt helpless, unaware of the details of her financial situation and feeling totally out of control. The Spendthrift Sally in her would have justified the need for spending it. But instead, Katie called me to discuss her options and the potential consequences of her choices. Feeling empowered and that she had a real choice, she made the decision to put some of the money towards her debt, some towards health expenses and a little just to splurge. New and improved Katie is now called, *"Facing-the-Facts Felicia"*.

You can create your own habits and rituals that you find to be most empowering for you. Here are some simple ideas and suggestions that you can implement daily, weekly, monthly, quarterly and annually.

Daily: Be conscious of every buying decision you make.

Whether it's a cup of coffee, or a special vacation. Make sure you truly value what you spend your money on. Before you buy, ask yourself, 'Will this move me closer to or further from my ultimate goals?'

Another great **daily ritual** to help you appreciate where you are and celebrate your successes, is to answer these two questions: "What are you grateful for?" and "What are your accomplishments?"

For over three years now, every single night before we go to bed, my husband and I have asked and answered these questions. As you can imagine, this ritual isn't just useful for our financial future. It's an ongoing effort that also continues to benefit our relationship every day.

Weekly: Begin tracking your Money MaSK™.

Yes, you won't have all the data until the end of the month, but it's better to make progress throughout the month than to leave it to the last minute. If you're using an online tracking program like mint.com or online banking, go through the uncategorized items and categorize them manually. If you're not using a program, pull up your weekly transactions from your bank account or credit card and keep a running tally per category.

Also, each week give yourself at least **one action item** to do for the week that will move you closer to one of your goals. Keep taking little action steps to move you forward.

Monthly: Track your net worth and Money MaSK™ and have a "Money Date."

Once you've gathered all the data, then have a money date (with you and your money) or if you you're in a relationship, have a money date with you, your money and your honey.

This money date is a chance for you to look at the numbers and evaluate the choices you've made over the last month. Then decide where to focus your attention in the upcoming month. Get clear on what targets you want to hit and make a game plan for how you will hit your targets.

Quarterly: Review your goals and evaluate.

Monitor your progress over the last quarter and tweak your goals or action steps as necessary, so that you continue to move in the right direction.

Annually: Look at your numbers over the past year. Celebrate and evaluate your progress.

If you haven't made much progress, that's a clear sign that you need help. Find someone who can help support you. You may need accountability to help you make the necessary changes, and a money coach is the best person to offer this. More on that in a moment.

Action Step:

What are you committed to doing? Write it down below:

DAILY	WEEKLY	MONTHLY	QUARTERLY	ANNUALLY

Well done! This is all coming together, isn't it?

4. Get Leverage

Remember Step 9? What were your reasons for changing? Why is it important to you that you continue this process? You need to be totally honest with yourself about what *could* happen if you don't take the appropriate action necessary to change.

Could you lose all your money? End up bankrupt? Lose your home? It can be really painful to think about these possibilities, but really understanding what your behaviors could lead to gives you enough leverage to take the positive steps you really need. Especially if they are uncomfortable.

Is setting aside an hour each month to track how much you make, spend, and keep really more painful for you than ruining your credit score for 7 years or getting evicted, or having no emergency fund, or borrowing money from your own kids? Keep this in mind when you want to quit.

If you ever stop following these steps, go back to chapter 9 and reconnect with the pain of not changing.

Action Step:

Here's the biggest reminder to myself of why I must change:
(Write it down now.)

_____

_____

_____

_____

Nice work! This will be a great reminder to you when you don't feel like doing something you know you need to do.

5. Cultivate a Wealthy Mindset

What and who you listen to, consume, and expose yourself to will influence your mindset. Imagine how you would begin to think if you were hanging out with successful people.

If you were to spend time with Sir Richard Branson (founder of Virgin records, billionaire and entrepreneur)—do you think you'd begin to believe that anything is possible?

If you had lunch with Oprah Winfrey (billionaire, actress, producer and philanthropist)— do you think you'd see the value of having wealth so you can give more and make a bigger difference?

If Donald Trump (billionaire, real estate mogul and reality TV star) took you on his private jet, do you think you'd start to see how great it is to dream BIG?

Most likely, you don't have the opportunity to hang out with these wealthy icons, but who do you know who has more abundance in their life than you do? How can you surround yourself with more successful people? Start spending time with money-minded peers and people who have had some level of (or are working toward), financial success. Just being around them can help introduce you to new concepts and ideas and shift your mindset.

One of the reasons that I have my TV show, *The Financial G-Spot*, on the Whatever it Takes Network is to surround myself and associate with other like-minded successful people.

Even if you can't hang out with wealthy people, you can read their books and articles, participate in their programs, or buy their products. You can easily find ways soak in their tips and advice.

This is why I've spent tens of thousands of dollars on seminars, programs and products. Even if my mentors don't know me from Adam, I know so much about who they are and how they think. This helps me maintain a wealthy mindset and abundant mentality.

There has never been so much information available as there is today. It's time to tune into a new station—so you can play a much bigger game.

Action Step:

Who are your new role models for a wealthy mindset?

Write some down now.

PEERS	TEACHERS/COACHES	EXPERTS/ICONS

Look at you go, you action-taker you! Awesome job!

6. Work with a Money Coach

Brenda, Sarah Jane, Matt, Katie and I were able to make progress so quickly because of one thing we had in common. Each and every one of us asked for help. We realized that our old patterns were moving us farther and farther away from the life that we wanted and we reached out and asked for help from a money coach.

It's always easier to get where you want to go when you have an expert to guide you and help you find the shortest path to success. It baffles me that most people don't hire coaches and mentors to help them with something as important as money - which can often dictate the quality of their lives.

If your roof leaks, and you need a new one, you probably wouldn't think twice about hiring a roofer. You wouldn't hire a hairdresser to fix your roof and unless you've got some serious roof repairing skills, you probably wouldn't try to fix it yourself. You'd hire the appropriate expert to help you solve the problem in the quickest amount of time. (If you are a roofer or a super fix-it-yourself type, insert your own appropriate metaphor here—i.e. if you're being sued and need a lawyer, looking for a home and need a realtor, etc.)

But when it comes to money problems, most people don't even think of hiring a money coach. At best, they may hire a Certified Financial Planner™, (or a financial advisor). The problem is, as I've discussed, CFP®s and financial advisors aren't taught to help you shift your beliefs. They're not taught to help you change your behaviors. Their job (again, I know this because I'm one of them) is to help you invest the money you already have. Hopefully, they have strategies to not just grow, but also to protect the money you've worked so hard to save. But if you don't have much to invest or what you really need are some serious belief and behavioral shifts, traditional financial service providers aren't going to help you much.

If you want money mastery and guidance along the way, hire a money coach.

A money coach gives you accountability and helps you recognize the patterns that are holding you back. They use a proven system and process to help **you** make changes, so you can transform your life. They expect the best from you but also bring to your attention troublesome behaviors or thought patterns that you might not see yourself.

Tiger Woods is the best golfer in the world, but he has a golf coach who can closely observe his swing and see problems he can't see— for instance, his golf coach might notice that his thumb was slightly to the left of where it should have been. Making one little shift with his thumb could change the trajectory of the ball, which could mean the difference between winning or not winning the PGA Tour.

A money coach can help you make small shifts that can change the trajectory of your life.

In addition, because the process of tracking your money and changing your behaviors will be uncomfortable, a money coach's job is to continue to remind you to push through those challenges. Some days, you won't feel like doing this, and life might get in the way as it always does at one time or another.

A money coach will help hold you accountable and keep you motivated. He or she will likely be able to relate to your situation (either personally or through other clients' experiences), and knows what it takes to get you to the next level of financial improvement. It's a money coach's job to pull you over to the other side of being in control of your money and ultimately help you transform your situation.

It's a money coach's job to help you change your beliefs and behaviors so you can get out of debt, get rid of money stress and save more, so then you can make money work for you!

You may remember my story from the beginning of the book that demonstrates how quickly you can change your financial situation from helpless to hopeful with the support of a money coach.

When I started out as a financial advisor almost 10 years ago, I brought in about $2,000 per month. Being a financial advisor with a poverty level income and a pile of debt felt totally incongruent to me. Even though my clients didn't know my exact situation, I felt embarrassed, I felt like a liar and I felt like I had no right to guide them. I so badly wanted to help people and since I could relate to people having struggles with money, I especially wanted to help them turn their financial situation around or get on track for their future goals.

I knew **I** needed to change.

I had leverage. I had motivation. But, I also had no clue how to make more money and build my wealth. When I had the opportunity to work with my money coach, Jeff, I was extremely scared. Even before speaking with him, I knew I couldn't "afford" it. I put that in quotes, because yes, I didn't have any extra money to go towards a coach, but the truth was, I couldn't "afford" **not** to hire him. I was digging myself into a deeper and deeper hole. I was wasting precious time and effort *trying* to help people, *trying* to fix my situation, but failing miserably.

I had to find a way to work with Jeff, because I knew that I was ready to change, but I desperately needed help. And frankly, I was impatient. I didn't want to make another $1,000 a month, or just get by. I wanted to make 6 figures and build my wealth as fast as possible so I could help others do the same.

Even though there were other coaches that I thought *might* be able to help me, I wanted the best. I was smart enough to know that hiring someone else at half the price was actually way more expensive in the long run, because I didn't think they'd be able to help me as much or as fast as Jeff would. He was 28 years old and had already made millions. He was my guy.

My first payment to Jeff was $800, equal to 40% of my monthly gross income!

I had to go further into debt to hire him and I'm grateful everyday that I took the leap of faith and believed in myself enough to do it. While this may seem like an odd thing for a Money Coach/Certified Financial Planner™/Wealth Strategist to advocate, I still wholeheartedly believe this:

The best investment in life, is in yourself.

No mutual fund, stock, real estate property or paid down debt is a better investment than *you*.

My coach taught me how to be the best at what I do.

I learned how to provide more value to my clients and in turn, was able to charge more for my services. I went from getting paid next-to-nothing for my time, to becoming highly paid and more importantly highly valued—without ever feeling like I had to "sell" people and without feeling bad about my fees.

Jeff taught me how to give so much value to my clients so that whatever the fee they paid, I was always able to show them how to make or save a multiple of that fee. This way, everyone got to win.

My clients were raving fans and I no longer felt incongruent or embarrassed, since after 18 months of working with him, I hit 6-figures.

Still my coach today, Jeffrey Slayter is a huge success. He's worked with over 3 million people in 12 countries worldwide, and has shared the stage with other global leaders like Sir Richard Branson, Tim Ferriss and Tony Robbins.

My decision to hire the *right* money coach is the reason that I have the success I have today.

If you now recognize that it's *you* who needs to change—not your boss, not your spouse, not your investments—then getting help is the quickest path to success.

You might ask whether a friend, parent, sibling, or spouse could serve as your coach and help hold you accountable. While a lovely idea in theory, your loved ones likely want you to be safe and comfortable and usually aren't in a position to push you out of your comfort zone. Also, they may not have the knowledge, skill or experience to help you get to where you want to be.

For example, in my case, I've always strived for more, but my mom tends to try to protect me, making sure that I'm safe and secure. She'd say things like, "Don't work too hard," or "Give yourself a break" or "Just relax." While my mom will always be a role model in my life, she'd attest to the fact that she'd be a horrific money coach.

When people want to advance to a higher level in any domain of life, whether it be around fitness, personal growth, or finance, we tend to put our foot on the brake instead of the gas when we hit a bump in the road. The people around us will unconsciously reinforce that tendency because they think (consciously or unconsciously) they are helping us and protecting us from getting hurt. But if you were to have a copilot there by your side, telling you to crank it up to lightning speed, you could break through to the next level.

So, be cautious when hiring a money coach. Anyone can call themselves a money coach, so you need to make sure you work with someone who has gotten results that you want, so they can help you get the results you want in the quickest amount of time.

To get the **"Top Ten Tips to Hiring a Money Coach"**, go to www.hireamoneycoach.com.

By the way, I'm not saying it's impossible to do it on your own. Maybe you can. But even if you could make huge progress on your own, I strongly believe that hiring a *great* money coach will save you a ton of time and money and give you exponential results. Don't think about how much it costs to work with someone. Think about how much it really costs you not to work with someone. Imagine if you not only had better habits and were able to make more, spend less and keep more but also—if you felt in control of your money and didn't feel stressed… what would that be worth to you?

Action Step:

Who will help support you in your success?

Do this now and take fast action. You can always make it better later.

MONEY COACH	PRODUCT/PROGRAM	FINANCIAL PLANNER

You can also take advantage of this free workshop.
www.RobynCrane.com/freeworkshop

Again, you are awesome! You are really setting yourself up for success now!

7. Take One Step at a Time

One of the challenges to anticipate, as I mentioned above, is the possibility of overwhelm. For some of you, the information in this book may be totally new. For others it may be in line with what you've heard before. Regardless of where you are, the best way to continue along the path of success is to just take the next step.

As long as you keep moving forward, nothing can hold you back.

As you apply the 10 simple steps you learned in this book, you'll begin to get the results that you *absolutely* desire and deserve and I'm confident that you will transform your life.

You deserve to have more freedom. You deserve to have more security. You deserve to have money mastery. Remember you and *only you* controls your own financial destiny.

I am so excited and happy for you to embark on this journey. To go from wherever you are to wherever you want to be.

As the Chinese philosopher Lao-tzu said,

"A journey of a thousand miles begins with a single step."

So here's all you need to do next.

Take one step now.

One small action, one little baby step after another. Then watch the life you want begin to unfold.

I'm so grateful to be apart of your journey. I can't wait to hear about your success.

Let me be the first to welcome you to your new life.

Your friend,
Robyn

If you'd like help from me personally, you can reach me at info@robyncrane.com, or simply call 1-800-273-1625.

REASONS OR RESULTS?

"When the moment of truth comes, you'll have one of two things:
1. Results you are proud of, or 2. Reasons why you didn't do it.
Are you ready for your breakthrough?
I created these interactive resources to help you:

http://robyncrane.com/bookbonuses

CONNECT WITH ROBYN

I don't know about you, but I LOVE how social media enables us to connect! Can you do me a favor?

Please pick *at least 2* of your favorite media channels, and leave me a message about what you got out of this book.

If you have any questions, I'd be glad to answer those as well.

I'll do my best to respond quickly and personally to <u>every single question</u>.

(All I ask is for your patience, as sometimes it may take a little time for me to reply. ☺)

Facebook:
https://www.facebook.com/moneyandrelationships
LinkedIn: https://www.linkedin.com/in/robyncrane
Twitter: https://twitter.com/robynhcrane
TV Show: http://financialgspot.com
Radio Show: http://robyncrane.com/radio-shows
YouTube: https://www.youtube.com/user/RobynHCrane
My Website: http://robyncrane.com/

FREE RESOURCES

THE MONEY MASTERY WORKSHOP:
Register for your free workshop now:

www.robyncrane.com/freeworkshop

BOOK BONUSES AND TEMPLATES:
Get all the book bonuses here:

www.robyncrane.com/bookbonuses

MONEY & RELATIONSHIP QUIZ:
Take the quiz, "Is Your Relationship in the RED?"

www.robyncrane.com/quiz

MONEY TYPE QUIZ:
Take the Money Type Quiz & watch the Money Type Videos.

www.RobynCrane.com/moneytypequiz

RICHER RELATIONSHIP GUIDEBOOK:
Download "The 4 Keys to a Richer Relationship"

www.RicherRelationship.com

VIDEO UPDATES:
Subscribe to my YouTube Channel

www.youtube.com/user/robynhcrane

WHAT TO DO NEXT

First, let me start by congratulating you on how far you've come.

You have to take a moment to really be proud of yourself because most never make it this far. Everyone loves to talk about all the big things they want to do, but few have the true passion and desire to do whatever it takes to get it. This book is just step one of the process to money mastery. If you'll allow me, I'd love to be your personal money coach and lead you through the entire process.

There are three major next steps that will allow you to work with me, and my team much more closely.

Step #1 – Claim Your Free Money Mastery Workshop ($497 Value)

Please immediately go to:
http://www.robyncrane.com/freeworkshop and register right away! It's absolutely free and all it takes is an email to register.

This free money mastery workshop consists of trainings where I will again walk you through the entire system, but this time you'll get to see me going through it with you! Watch and learn as I interact with you regarding all the ins and outs of how this relates to your life. You'll also get to meet our successful friends and clients that I've worked with, and you'll have an opportunity to ask any questions you may have.

*This is your opportunity to join our community of incredible people who want to raise the bar in their lives. Imagine being surrounded by awesome like-minded people just like you! You can get all of this for free. Even if you missed our LIVE presentations, I am going to make the replays available for a limited time only. The replays are also free and you can watch them at your own pace.

Step #2 – Go Get Your Free Book Bonuses (priceless)

To get then now, go to: http://www.robyncrane.com/bookbonuses
Again, this is absolutely free, simple, fast and easy.

<u>Step #3 – Do The Exercises In This Book!</u>

Maybe you skipped to the end of this book, and you haven't
completed the exercises in the book yet. Or maybe you thought
you'd go back and do them later… either way GO BACK and
complete them one by one. They will serve you well, I promise.

The future you really want is just around the corner for you. You
can start building a life of true financial freedom starting today. All
you need to do is officially declare it and then follow the entire
system exactly. That's it. So if you're ready, I am too, lets get
going!

I wish you the very best. I wish you millions in profit and a life full
of nothing but your dreams coming true. If I can personally do
anything to help you achieve that, you know where to find me.
Looking forward to our journey together!

WORKING WITH ROBYN

MONEY COACHING

I have the fantastic opportunity to work with people who want to improve their financial situation and get further ahead financially. I love it!

I work with people in small groups, as couples, or sometimes one-on-one—it all depends on what's right for you. Regardless of the amount of money you have, *money coaching* is for you if are finally ready to do whatever it takes to claim the quality of life you deserve.

For more details and to inquire about money coaching email: support@robyncrane.com with the subject line: Money Coaching with Robyn.

PRIVATE WORKSHOPS AND SEMINARS

The only thing I like better than coaching, is speaking to groups! I am *passionate* about helping as many people as possible overcome their money issues and have a phenomenal life.

My workshops and seminars are structured to give you an interactive experience. You won't sit there passively at one of my programs, they are designed to help you jumpstart your new life and gain the momentum you need to pursue your financial and relationship goals!

For more details: www.RobynCrane.com/

PUBLIC SPEAKING

If you would like to recommend me to speak at an organization, corporation, school, church or synagogue, please email booking@robyncrane.com.

Please include "SPEAKING ENGAGEMENT" in the subject line. In certain situations, I can be persuaded to speak pro-bono... especially if you know of a group, organization or cause that I may want to support. Please reach out. I can't always say yes, but I'd love to hear from you.

For more details, a downloadable media kit, and speaker reels visit: www.RobynCrane.com/speaking

BOOK ROBYN

WOULD YOU LIKE ROBYN TO SPEAK AT YOUR COMPANY OR ORGANIZATION?

HOT TOPICS

Unconventional Wisdom For Women
- How To Use The "Crazy 8 of Success,"
so you can have your Financial Breakthrough

The Belief Loan Phenomenon
- How To Borrow Beliefs To
Shortcut Your Way to Success

The Financial Sweet Spot
- How to Get High Paying Clients With
A Proven Sales System

Master Your Money, Accelerate Your Success
- How To Improve Your Money Habits
To Breakthrough In Your Life

The ABC's of Money Parenting™
- How to Raise Confident, Successful Kids Who Grow
Up to Be RICH™ (Responsible, In Control, and Happy)

*"I look forward to helping you, and
your group - get right on the money."*

-- Robyn Crane

CONTACT ROBYN

800-273-1625
booking@RobynCrane.com

ABOUT THE AUTHOR

Money coach and wealth strategist, Robyn Crane is the host of the TV show, The *Financial G-Spot*, the radio show, *Let's Talk Money* and #1 Best Selling Author. Her blueprint for financial and relationship success has been featured on Fox Business News, The Motley Fool and SavingsAccount.com.

From years of experience as a Certified Financial Planner™ practitioner, coupled with her unique background as a touring singer-songwriter, Robyn provides invaluable content in a most captivating and entertaining way. Be it readers of her books or articles, participants in her programs, or attendees at her seminars, audiences are inspired by Robyn to let their guards down about money and take fast action. She introduces humor in the complex web of money and relationships and helps you find your "financial g-spot", so you can reach financial ecstasy.

Robyn has merged both the strategy and psychology of money to create works such as Money Parenting™ (How to raise financially responsible kids by leading by example) and the KYM GYM System™ (Know Your Money to Grow Your Money). With these powerful strategies, Robyn helps people overcome their money issues and improve the quality of their lives -- every day.

In addition to her books and programs, Robyn is an engaging and in-demand speaker who is regularly invited to speak at companies, women's conferences, chambers of commerce, entrepreneurial groups and various types of organizations around the country.

Robyn is currently at work on her next book about how money affects intimate relationships. Her current working title is, *The Ménage à Trois: How to Prevent the 3-Way Between You, Your Money & Your Honey from Ruining Your Relationship.*

Visit www.RicherRelationship.com to get the key principles of Robyn's forthcoming book and be notified of its release.

LEGAL NOTICES

The information presented herein represents the view of the author as of the date of publication. Because of the rate with which conditions change, the author reserves the right to alter and update her opinion based on new conditions. This book is for informational purposes only. While every attempt has been made to verify the information provided in this book, neither the author nor her affiliates/partners assume any responsibility for errors, inaccuracies or omissions. Any slights of people or organizations are unintentional. If advice concerning legal, financial or any other related matters are needed, the services of a fully qualified professional should be sought. This book is not intended for use as a source of legal advice.

STATEMENT OF EARNINGS/DISCLAIMER

Every effort has been made to accurately represent the information in this book. Examples in these materials are not to be interpreted as a promise or guarantee of earnings or investment growth. Wealth accumulation is entirely dependent on the person using our product, ideas and techniques. We do not purport this as a "get rich scheme." Your level of success in attaining the results claimed in this material depends on the time you devote to the program, ideas and techniques mentioned, your finances, knowledge and various skills. Since these factors differ according to individuals, we cannot guarantee your financial success. Nor are we responsible for any of your actions.

Made in the USA
Middletown, DE
12 May 2021